Ecofascism
Lessons from the German Experience

Janet Biehl & Peter Staudenmaier

Library of Congress Cataloguing-in-Publication Data

Biehl, Janet, 1953–
     Ecofascism: lessons from the German experience / by Janet
Biehl and Peter Staudenmaier
     p. cm.
     Includes bibliographical references.
     ISBN 1-873176 73 2 (paper)
     1. Green movement—Germany—History—20th cen-
tury. 2. Fascism-- Germany. 3. Environmental policy—
Germany. 4. Environmentalism. 5. Political policy—
Germany—History. 6. Right and left (Political science) 7.
Grünen (Political party) I. Staudenmaier, Peter, 1965- .
II. Title
HC79.E5B5   1995
304.2'0943'—dc20   95-40752
                                                          CIP

British Library Cataloguing in Publication Data

A catalogue record for this title is available from the
British Library.

First published in 1995 by

AK Press   AK Press
22 Lutton Place   P.O. Box 40682
Edinburgh, Scotland   San Francisco, CA
EH8 9PE   94140-0682

Typeset and design donated by Freddie Baer.

CONTENTS

INTRODUCTION

For most compassionate and humane people today, the ecological crisis is a source of major concern. Not only do many ecological activists struggle to eliminate toxic wastes, to preserve tropical rainforests and old-growth redwoods, and to roll back the destruction of the biosphere, but many ordinary people in all walks of life are intensely concerned about the nature of the planet that their children will grow up to inhabit. In Europe as in the United States, most ecological activists think of themselves as socially progressive. That is, they also support demands of oppressed peoples for social justice and believe that the needs of human beings living in poverty, illness, warfare, and famine also require our most serious attention.

For many such people, it may come as a surprise to learn that the history of ecological politics has not always been inherently and necessarily progressive and benign. In fact, ecological ideas have a history of being distorted and placed in the service of highly regressive ends—even of fascism itself. As Peter Staudenmaier shows in the first essay in this pamphlet, important tendencies in German "ecologism," which has long roots in nineteenth-century nature mysticism, fed into the rise of Nazism in the twentieth century. During the Third Reich, Staudenmaier goes on to show, Nazi "ecologists" even made organic farming, vegetarianism, nature worship, and related themes into key elements not only in their ideology but in their governmental policies. Moreover, Nazi "ecological" ideology was used to justify the destruction of European Jewry. Yet some of the themes that Nazi ideologists articulated bear an uncomfortably close resemblance to themes familiar to ecologically concerned people today.

As social ecologists, it is not our intention to deprecate the all-important efforts that environmentalists and ecologists are making to rescue the biosphere from destruction. Quite to the contrary: It is our deepest concern to preserve the integrity of serious ecological movements from ugly reactionary tendencies that seek to exploit the widespread popular concern about ecological problems for regressive agendas. But we find that the "ecological scene" of our time—with its growing mysticism and antihumanism—poses serious problems about the direction in which the ecology movement will go.

In most Western nations in the late twentieth century, expressions of racism and anti-immigrant sentiments are not only increasingly voiced but increasingly tolerated. Equally disconcertingly, fascist ideologists and political groups are experiencing a resurgence as well. Updating their ideology and speaking the new language of ecology, these movements are once again invoking ecological themes to serve social reaction. In ways that sometimes approximate beliefs of progressive-minded ecologists, these reactionary and outright fascist ecologists emphasize the supremacy of the "Earth" over people; evoke "feelings" and intuition at the expense of reason; and uphold a crude sociobiologistic and even Malthusian biologism. Tenets of "New Age" eco-ideology that seem benign to most people in England and the United States—specifically, its mystical and antirational strains—are being intertwined with ecofascism in Germany today. Janet Biehl's essay explores this hijacking of ecology for racist, nationalistic, and fascist ends.

Taken together, these essays examine aspects of German fascism, past and present, in order to draw lessons from them for ecology movements both in Germany and elsewhere. Despite its singularities, the German experience offers a clear warning against the misuse of ecology, in a world that seems ever more willing to tolerate movements and ideologies once regarded as despicable and obsolete. Political ecology thinkers have yet to fully examine the political implications of these ideas in the English-speaking world as well as in Germany.

What prevents ecological politics from yielding reaction or fascism with an ecological patina is an ecology movement that maintains a broad social emphasis, one that places the ecological crisis in a social context. As social ecologists, we see the roots of the present ecological crisis in an irrational society—not in the biological makeup of human beings, nor in a particular religion, nor in reason, science, or technology. On the contrary, we uphold the importance of reason, science, and technology in creating both a progressive ecological movement and an ecological society. It is a specific set of social relations—above all, the competitive market economy—that is presently destroying the biosphere. Mysticism and biologism, at the very least, deflect public attention away from such *social* causes. In presenting these essays, we are trying to preserve the all-important progressive and emancipatory implications of ecological politics. More than ever, an ecological commitment requires people today to avoid repeating the errors of the past, lest the ecology movement become absorbed in the mystical and antihumanistic trends that abound today.

J.B.
P.S.

Fascist Ecology:
The "Green Wing" of the Nazi Party and its Historical Antecedents

Peter Staudenmaier

"We recognize that separating humanity from nature, from the whole of life, leads to humankind's own destruction and to the death of nations. Only through a reintegration of humanity into the whole of nature can our people be made stronger. That is the fundamental point of the biological tasks of our age. Humankind alone is no longer the focus of thought, but rather life as a whole . . . This striving toward connectedness with the totality of life, with nature itself, a nature into which we are born, this is the deepest meaning and the true essence of National Socialist thought."[1]

In our zeal to condemn the status quo, radicals often carelessly toss about epithets like "fascist" and "ecofascist," thus contributing to a sort of conceptual inflation that in no way furthers effective social critique. In such a situation, it is easy to overlook the fact that there are still virulent strains of fascism in our political culture which, however marginal, demand our attention. One of the least recognized or understood of these strains is the phenomenon one might call "actually existing ecofascism," that is, the preoccupation of authentically fascist movements with environmentalist concerns. In order to grasp the peculiar intensity and endurance of this affiliation, we would do well to examine more closely its most notorious historical incarnation, the so-called "green wing" of German National Socialism.

Despite an extensive documentary record, the subject remains an elusive one, underappreciated by professional historians and environmental activists alike. In English-speaking countries as well as in Germany itself, the very existence of a "green wing" in the Nazi movement, much less its inspiration, goals, and consequences, has yet to be adequately researched and analyzed. Most of the handful of available interpretations succumb to either an alarming intellectual affinity with their subject[2] or a naive refusal to examine the full extent of the "ideological overlap between nature conservation and National Socialism."[3] This article presents a brief and necessarily schematic overview of the ecological components of Nazism, emphasizing both their central role in Nazi ideology and their practical implementation during the Third Reich. A preliminary survey of nineteenth and twentieth century precursors to classical ecofascism should serve to illuminate the conceptual underpinnings common to all forms of reactionary ecology.

Two initial clarifications are in order. First, the terms "environmental" and "ecological" are here used more or less interchangeably to denote ideas, attitudes, and practices commonly associated with the contemporary environmental movement. This is not an anachronism; it simply indicates an interpretive approach which highlights connections to present-day concerns. Second, this approach is not meant to endorse the historiographically discredited notion that pre-1933 historical data can or should be read as "leading inexorably" to the Nazi calamity. Rather, our concern here is with discerning ideological continuities and tracing political genealogies, in an attempt to understand the past in light of our current situation — to make history relevant to the present social and ecological crisis.

THE ROOTS OF THE BLOOD AND SOIL MYSTIQUE

Germany is not only the birthplace of the science of ecology and the site of Green politics' rise to prominence; it has also been home to a peculiar synthesis of naturalism and nationalism forged under the influence of the Romantic tradition's anti-Enlightenment irrationalism. Two nineteenth century figures exemplify this ominous conjunction: Ernst Moritz Arndt and Wilhelm Heinrich Riehl.

While best known in Germany for his fanatical nationalism, Arndt was also dedicated to the cause of the peasantry, which lead him to a concern for the welfare of the land itself. Historians of German environmentalism mention him as the earliest example of 'ecological' thinking in the modern sense.[4] His remarkable 1815 article *On the Care and Conservation of Forests*, written at the dawn of industrialization in Central Europe, rails against shortsighted exploitation of woodlands and soil, condemning deforestation and its economic causes. At times he wrote in terms strikingly similar to those of contemporary biocentrism: "When one sees nature in a necessary connectedness and inter-relationship, then all things are equally important — shrub, worm, plant, human, stone, nothing first or last, but all one single unity."[5]

Arndt's environmentalism, however, was inextricably bound up with virulently xenophobic nationalism. His eloquent and prescient appeals for ecological sensitivity were couched always in terms of the well-being of the *German* soil and the *German* people, and his repeated lunatic polemics against miscegenation, demands for teutonic racial purity, and epithets against the French, Slavs, and Jews marked every aspect of his thought. At the very outset of the nineteenth century the deadly connection between love of land and militant racist nationalism was firmly set in place.

Riehl, a student of Arndt, further developed this sinister tradition. In some respects his 'green' streak went significantly deeper than Arndt's; presaging certain tendencies in recent environmental activism, his 1853 essay *Field and Forest* ended with a call to fight for "the rights of wilderness." But even here nationalist pathos set the tone: "We must save the forest, not only so that our ovens do not become cold in winter, but also so that the pulse of life of the people continues to beat warm and joyfully, so that Germany remains German."[6] Riehl was an implacable opponent of the rise of industrialism and urbanization; his overtly antisemitic glorification of rural peasant values and undifferentiated condemnation of modernity established him as the "founder of agrarian romanticism and anti-urbanism."[7]

These latter two fixations matured in the second half of the nineteenth century in the context of the *völkisch* movement, a powerful cultural disposition and social tendency which united ethnocentric populism with nature mysticism. At the heart of the *völkisch* temptation was a pathological response to modernity. In the face of the very real dislocations brought on by the triumph of industrial capitalism and national unification, *völkisch* thinkers preached a return to the land, to the simplicity and wholeness of a life attuned to nature's purity. The mystical effusiveness of this perverted utopianism was matched by its political vulgarity. While "the Volkish movement aspired to reconstruct the society that was sanctioned by history, rooted in nature, and in communion with the cosmic life spirit,"[8] it pointedly refused to locate the sources of alienation, rootlessness and environmental destruction in social structures, laying the blame instead to rationalism, cosmopolitanism, and urban civilization. The stand-in for all of these was the age-old object of peasant hatred and middle-class resentment: the Jews. "The Germans were in search of a mysterious wholeness that would restore them to primeval happiness, destroying the hostile milieu of urban industrial civilization that the Jewish conspiracy had foisted on them."[9]

Reformulating traditional German antisemitism into nature-friendly terms, the *völkisch* movement carried a volatile amalgam of nineteenth century cultural prejudices, Romantic obsessions with purity, and anti-Enlightenment sentiment into twentieth century political discourse. The emergence of modern ecology forged the final link in the fateful chain which bound together aggressive nationalism, mystically charged racism, and environmentalist predilections. In 1867 the German zoologist Ernst Haeckel coined the term 'ecology' and began to establish it as a scientific discipline dedicated to studying the interactions between organism and environment. Haeckel was also the chief popularizer of Darwin and evolutionary theory for the German-speaking world, and developed a peculiar sort of social darwinist philosophy he called 'monism.' The German Monist League he founded combined scientifically based ecological holism with *völkisch* social views. Haeckel believed in nordic racial superiority, strenuously opposed race mixing and enthusiastically supported racial eugenics. His fervent nationalism became fanatical with the onset of World War I, and he fulminated in antisemitic tones against the post-war Council Republic in Bavaria.

In this way "Haeckel contributed to that special variety of German thought which served as the seed bed for National Socialism. He became one of Germany's major ideologists for racism, nationalism and imperialism."[10] Near the end of his life he joined the Thule Society, "a secret, radically right-wing organization which played a key role in the establishment of the Nazi movement."[11] But more than merely personal continuities are at stake here. The pioneer of scientific ecology, along with his disciples Willibald Hentschel, Wilhelm Bölsche and Bruno Wille, profoundly shaped the thinking of subsequent generations of environmentalists by embedding concern for the natural world in a tightly woven web of regressive social themes. From its very beginnings, then, ecology was bound up in an intensely reactionary political framework.

The specific contours of this early marriage of ecology and authoritarian social views are highly instructive. At the center of this ideological complex is the direct, unmediated application of biological categories to the social realm. Haeckel held that "civilization and the life of nations are governed by the same laws as prevail throughout nature and organic life."[12] This notion of 'natural laws' or 'natural order' has long been a mainstay of reactionary environmental thought. Its concomitant is anti-humanism:

> Thus, for the Monists, perhaps the most pernicious feature of European bourgeois civilization was the inflated importance which it attached to the idea of man in general, to his existence and to his talents, and to the belief that through his unique rational faculties man could essentially recreate the world and bring about a universally more harmonious and ethically just social

order. [Humankind was] an insignificant creature when viewed as part of and measured against the vastness of the cosmos and the overwhelming forces of nature.[13]

Other Monists extended this anti-humanist emphasis and mixed it with the traditional *völkisch* motifs of indiscriminate anti-industrialism and anti-urbanism as well as the newly emerging pseudo-scientific racism. The linchpin, once again, was the conflation of biological and social categories. The biologist Raoul Francé, founding member of the Monist League, elaborated so-called *Lebensgesetze*, 'laws of life' through which the natural order determines the social order. He opposed racial mixing, for example, as "unnatural." Francé is acclaimed by contemporary ecofascists as a "pioneer of the ecology movement."[14]

Francé's colleague Ludwig Woltmann, another student of Haeckel, insisted on a biological interpretation for all societal phenomena, from cultural attitudes to economic arrangements. He stressed the supposed connection between environmental purity and 'racial' purity: "Woltmann took a negative attitude toward modern industrialism. He claimed that the change from an agrarian to an industrial society had hastened the decline of the race. In contrast to nature, which engendered the harmonic forms of Germanism, there were the big cities, diabolical and inorganic, destroying the virtues of the race."[15]

Thus by the early years of the twentieth century a certain type of 'ecological' argumentation, saturated with right-wing political content, had attained a measure of respectability within the political culture of Germany. During the turbulent period surrounding World War I, the mixture of ethnocentric fanaticism, regressive rejection of modernity and genuine environmental concern proved to be a very potent potion indeed.

THE YOUTH MOVEMENT AND THE WEIMAR ERA

The chief vehicle for carrying this ideological constellation to prominence was the youth movement, an amorphous phenomenon which played a decisive but highly ambivalent role in shaping German popular culture during the first three tumultuous decades of this century. Also known as the *Wandervögel* (which translates roughly as 'wandering free spirits'), the youth movement was a hodge-podge of countercultural elements, blending neo-Romanticism, Eastern philosophies, nature mysticism, hostility to reason, and a strong communal impulse in a confused but no less ardent search for authentic, non-alienated social relations. Their back-to-the-land emphasis spurred a passionate sensitivity to the natural world and the damage it suffered. They have been aptly characterized as 'right-wing hippies,' for although some sectors of the movement gravitated toward various forms of emancipatory politics (though usually shedding their environmentalist trappings in the process), most of the *Wandervögel* were eventually absorbed by the Nazis. This shift from nature worship to *Führer* worship is worth examining.

The various strands of the youth movement shared a common self-conception: they were a purportedly 'non-political' response to a deep cultural crisis, stressing the primacy of direct emotional experience over social critique and action. They pushed the contradictions of their time to the breaking point, but were unable or unwilling to take the final step toward organized, focused social rebellion, "convinced that the changes they wanted to effect in society could not be brought about by political means, but only by the improvement of the individual."[16] This proved to be a fatal error. "Broadly speaking, two ways of revolt were open to them: they could have pursued their radical critique of society, which in due course would have brought them into the camp of social revolution. [But] the *Wandervögel* chose the other form of protest against society — romanticism."[17]

This posture lent itself all too readily to a very different kind of political mobilization: the 'unpolitical' zealotry of fascism. The youth movement did not simply fail in its chosen form of protest, it was actively realigned when its members went over to the Nazis by the thousands. Its countercultural energies and its dreams of harmony with nature bore the bitterest fruit. This is, perhaps, the unavoidable trajectory of any movement which acknowledges and opposes social and ecological problems but does not recognize their systemic roots or actively resist the political and economic structures which generate them. Eschewing societal transformation in favor of personal change, an ostensibly apolitical disaffection can, in times of crisis, yield barbaric results.

The attraction such perspectives exercised on idealistic youth is clear: the enormity of the crisis seemed to enjoin a total rejection of its apparent causes. It is in the specific form of this rejection that the danger lies. Here the work of several more theoretical minds from the period is instructive. The philosopher Ludwig Klages profoundly influenced the youth movement and particularly shaped their ecological consciousness. He authored a tremendously important essay titled "Man and Earth" for the legendary Meissner gathering of the *Wandervögel* in 1913.[18] An extraordinarily poignant text and the best known of all Klages' work, it is not only "one of the very greatest manifestoes of the radical ecopacifist movement in Germany,"[19] but also a classic example of the seductive terminology of reactionary ecology.

"Man and Earth" anticipated just about all of the themes of the contemporary ecology movement. It decried the accelerating extinction of species, disturbance of global ecosystemic balance, deforestation, destruction of aboriginal peoples and of wild habitats, urban sprawl, and the increasing alienation of people from nature. In emphatic terms it disparaged Christianity, capitalism, economic utilitarianism, hyperconsumption and the ideology of 'progress.' It even condemned the environmental destructiveness of rampant tourism and the slaughter of whales, and displayed a clear recognition of the planet as an ecological totality. All of this in 1913 !

It may come as a surprise, then, to learn that Klages was throughout his life politically archconservative and a venomous antisemite. One historian labels him a "Volkish fanatic" and another considers him simply "an intellectual pacemaker for the Third Reich" who "paved the way for fascist philosophy in many important respects."[20] In "Man and Earth" a genuine outrage at the devastation of the natural environment is coupled with a political subtext of cultural despair.[21] Klages' diagnosis of the ills of modern society, for all its declamations about capitalism, returns always to a single culprit: "Geist." His idiosyncratic use of this term, which means mind or intellect, was meant to denounce not only hyperrationalism or instrumental reason, but rational thought itself. Such a wholesale indictment of reason cannot help but have savage political implications. It forecloses any chance of rationally reconstructing society's relationship with nature and justifies the most brutal authoritarianism. But the lessons of Klages' life and work have been hard for ecologists to learn. In 1980, "Man and Earth" was republished as an esteemed and seminal treatise to accompany the birth of the German Greens.

Another philosopher and stern critic of Enlightenment who helped bridge fascism and environmentalism was Martin Heidegger. A much more renowned thinker than Klages, Heidegger preached "authentic Being" and harshly criticized modern technology, and is therefore often celebrated as a precursor of ecological thinking. On the basis of his critique of technology and rejection of humanism, contemporary deep ecologists have elevated Heidegger to their pantheon of eco-heroes:

> Heidegger's critique of anthropocentric humanism, his call for humanity to learn to "let things be," his notion that humanity is involved in a "play" or "dance" with earth, sky, and gods, his meditation on the possibility of an authentic mode of "dwelling" on the earth, his complaint that industrial technology is laying waste to the earth, his emphasis on the importance of local place and "homeland," his claim that humanity should guard and preserve things, instead of dominating them — all these aspects of Heidegger's thought help to support the claim that he is a major deep ecological theorist.[22]

Such effusions are, at best, dangerously naive. They suggest a style of thought utterly oblivious to the history of fascist appropriations of *all* the elements the quoted passage praises in Heidegger. (To his credit, the author of the above lines, a major deep ecological theorist in his own right, has since changed his position and eloquently urged his colleagues to do the same.)[23] As for the philosopher of Being himself, he was — unlike Klages, who lived in Switzerland after 1915 — an active member of the Nazi party and for a time enthusiastically, even adoringly supported the *Führer*. His mystical panegyrics to *Heimat* (home-land) were complemented by a deep antisemitism, and his metaphysically phrased broadsides against technology and modernity converged neatly with populist demagogy. Although he lived and taught for thirty years after the fall of the Third Reich, Heidegger never once publicly regretted, much less renounced, his involvement with National Socialism, nor even perfunctorily condemned its crimes. His work, whatever its philosophical merits, stands today as a signal admonition about the political uses of anti-humanism in ecological garb.

In addition to the youth movement and protofascist philosophies, there were, of course, practical efforts at protecting natural habitats during the Weimar period. Many of these projects were profoundly implicated in the ideology which culminated in the victory of 'Blood and Soil.' A 1923 recruitment pitch for a woodlands preservation outfit gives a sense of the environmental rhetoric of the time:

> "In every German breast the German forest quivers with its caverns and ravines, crags and boulders, waters and winds, legends and fairy tales, with its songs and its melodies, and awakens a powerful yearning and a longing for home; in all German souls the German forest lives and weaves with its depth and breadth, its stillness and strength, its might and dignity, its riches and its beauty — it is the source of German inwardness, of the German soul, of German freedom. Therefore protect and care for the German forest for the sake of the elders and the youth, and join the new German "League for the Protection and Consecration of the German Forest."[24]

The mantra-like repetition of the word "German" and the mystical depiction of the sacred forest fuse together, once again, nationalism and naturalism. This intertwinement took on a grisly significance with the collapse of the Weimar republic. For alongside such relatively innocuous conservation groups, another organization was growing which offered these ideas a hospitable home: the National Socialist German Workers Party, known by its acronym NSDAP. Drawing on the heritage of Arndt, Riehl,

Haeckel, and others (all of whom were honored between 1933 and 1945 as forebears of triumphant National Socialism), the Nazi movement's incorporation of environmentalist themes was a crucial factor in its rise to popularity and state power.

NATURE IN NATIONAL SOCIALIST IDEOLOGY

The reactionary ecological ideas whose outlines are sketched above exerted a powerful and lasting influence on many of the central figures in the NSDAP. Weimar culture, after all, was fairly awash in such theories, but the Nazis gave them a peculiar inflection. The National Socialist "religion of nature," as one historian has described it, was a volatile admixture of primeval teutonic nature mysticism, pseudo-scientific ecology, irrationalist anti-humanism, and a mythology of racial salvation through a return to the land. Its predominant themes were 'natural order,' organicist holism and denigration of humanity: "Throughout the writings, not only of Hitler, but of most Nazi ideologues, one can discern a fundamental deprecation of humans *vis-à-vis* nature, and, as a logical corollary to this, an attack upon human efforts to master nature."[25] Quoting a Nazi educator, the same source continues: "anthropocentric views in general had to be rejected. They would be valid only 'if it is assumed that nature has been created only for man. We decisively reject this attitude. According to our conception of nature, man is a link in the living chain of nature just as any other organism'."[26]

Such arguments have a chilling currency within contemporary ecological discourse: the key to social-ecological harmony is ascertaining "the eternal laws of nature's processes" (Hitler) and organizing society to correspond to them. The *Führer* was particularly fond of stressing the "helplessness of humankind in the face of nature's everlasting law."[27] Echoing Haeckel and the Monists, *Mein Kampf* announces: "When people attempt to rebel against the iron logic of nature, they come into conflict with the very same principles to which they owe their existence as human beings. Their actions against nature must lead to their own downfall."[28]

The authoritarian implications of this view of humanity and nature become even clearer in the context of the Nazis' emphasis on holism and organicism. In 1934 the director of the Reich Agency for Nature Protection, Walter Schoenichen, established the following objectives for biology curricula: "Very early, the youth must develop an understanding of the civic importance of the 'organism', i.e. the co-ordination of all parts and organs for the benefit of the one and superior task of life."[29] This (by now familiar) unmediated adaptation of biological concepts to social phenomena served to justify not only the totalitarian social order of the Third Reich but also the expansionist politics of *Lebensraum* (the plan of conquering 'living space' in Eastern Europe for the German people). It also provided the link between environmental purity and racial purity:

> Two central themes of biology education follow [according to the Nazis] from the holistic perspective: nature protection and eugenics. If one views nature as a unified whole, students will automatically develop a sense for ecology and environmental conservation. At the same time, the nature protection concept will direct attention to the urbanized and 'overcivilized' modern human race.[30]

In many varieties of the National Socialist world view ecological themes were linked with traditional agrarian romanticism and hostility to urban civilization, all revolving around the idea of rootedness in nature. This conceptual constellation, especially the search for a lost connection to nature, was most pronounced among the neo-pagan elements in the Nazi leadership, above all Heinrich Himmler, Alfred Rosenberg, and Walther Darré. Rosenberg wrote in his colossal *The Myth of the 20th Century:* "Today we see the steady stream from the countryside to the city, deadly for the *Volk.* The cities swell ever larger, unnerving the *Volk* and destroying the threads which bind humanity to nature; they attract adventurers and profiteers of all colors, thereby fostering racial chaos."[31]

Such musings, it must be stressed, were not mere rhetoric; they reflected firmly held beliefs and, indeed, practices at the very top of the Nazi hierarchy which are today conventionally associated with ecological attitudes. Hitler and Himmler were both strict vegetarians and animal lovers, attracted to nature mysticism and homeopathic cures, and staunchly opposed to vivisection and cruelty to animals. Himmler even established experimental organic farms to grow herbs for SS medicinal purposes. And Hitler, at times, could sound like a veritable Green utopian, discussing authoritatively and in detail various renewable energy sources (including environmentally appropriate hydropower and producing natural gas from sludge) as alternatives to coal, and declaring "water, winds and tides" as the energy path of the future.[32]

Even in the midst of war, Nazi leaders maintained their commitment to ecological ideals which were, for them, an essential element of racial rejuvenation. In December 1942, Himmler released a decree "On the Treatment of the Land in the Eastern Territories," referring to the newly annexed portions of Poland. It read in part:

> The peasant of our racial stock has always carefully endeavored to increase the natural powers of the soil, plants, and animals, and to preserve the balance of the whole of nature. For him, respect for divine creation is the measure of all culture. If, therefore, the new *Lebensräume* (living spaces) are to become a homeland for our settlers, the planned arrangement of the landscape to keep it close to nature is a decisive prerequisite. It is one of the bases for fortifying the German *Volk*.[33]

This passage recapitulates almost all of the tropes comprised by classical ecofascist ideology: *Lebensraum, Heimat,* the agrarian mystique, the health of the *Volk,* closeness to and respect for nature (explicitly constructed as the standard against which society is to be judged), maintaining nature's precarious balance, and the earthy powers of the soil and its creatures. Such motifs were anything but personal idiosyncracies on the part of Hitler, Himmler, or Rosenberg; even Göring — who was, along with Goebbels, the member of the Nazi inner circle least hospitable to ecological ideas — appeared at times to be a committed conservationist.[34] These sympathies were also hardly restricted to the upper echelons of the party. A study of the membership rolls of several mainstream Weimar era *Naturschutz* (nature protection) organizations revealed that by 1939, fully 60 percent of these conservationists had joined the NSDAP (compared to about 10 percent of adult men and 25 percent of teachers and lawyers).[35] Clearly the affinities between environmentalism and National Socialism ran deep.

At the level of ideology, then, ecological themes played a vital role in German fascism. It would be a grave mistake, however, to treat these elements as mere propaganda, cleverly deployed to mask Nazism's true character as a technocratic-industrialist juggernaut. The definitive history of German anti-urbanism and agrarian romanticism argues incisively against this view:

> Nothing could be more wrong than to suppose that most of the leading National Socialist ideologues had cynically feigned an agrarian romanticism and hostility to urban culture, without any inner conviction and for merely electoral and propaganda purposes, in order to hoodwink the public [. . .] In reality, the majority of the leading National Socialist ideologists were without any doubt more or less inclined to agrarian romanticism and anti-urbanism and convinced of the need for a relative re-agrarianization.[36]

The question remains, however: To what extent did the Nazis actually implement environmental policies during the twelve-year Reich? There is strong evidence that the 'ecological' tendency in the party, though largely ignored today, had considerable success for most of the party's reign. This "green wing" of the NSDAP was represented above all by Walther Darré, Fritz Todt, Alwin Seifert and Rudolf Hess, the four figures who primarily shaped fascist ecology in practice.

BLOOD AND SOIL AS OFFICIAL DOCTRINE

"The unity of blood and soil must be restored," proclaimed Richard Walther Darré in 1930.[37] This infamous phrase denoted a quasi-mystical connection between 'blood' (the race or *Volk*) and 'soil' (the land and the natural environment) specific to

Germanic peoples and absent, for example, among Celts and Slavs. For the enthusiasts of *Blut und Boden*, the Jews especially were a rootless, wandering people, incapable of any true relationship with the land. German blood, in other words, engendered an exclusive claim to the sacred German soil. While the term "blood and soil" had been circulating in *völkisch* circles since at least the Wilhelmine era, it was Darré who first popularized it as a slogan and then enshrined it as a guiding principle of Nazi thought. Harking back to Arndt and Riehl, he envisioned a thoroughgoing ruralization of Germany and Europe, predicated on a revitalized yeoman peasantry, in order to ensure racial health and ecological sustainability.

Darré was one of the party's chief "race theorists" and was also instrumental in galvanizing peasant support for the Nazis during the critical period of the early 1930s. From 1933 until 1942 he held the posts of Reich Peasant Leader and Minister of Agriculture. This was no minor fiefdom; the agriculture ministry had the fourth largest budget of all the myriad Nazi ministries even well into the war.[38] From this position Darré was able to lend vital support to various ecologically oriented initiatives. He played an essential part in unifying the nebulous proto-environmentalist tendencies in National Socialism:

> It was Darré who gave the ill-defined anti-civilization, anti-liberal, anti-modern and latent anti-urban sentiments of the Nazi elite a foundation in the agrarian mystique. And it seems as if Darré had an immense influence on the ideology of National Socialism, as if he was able to articulate significantly more clearly than before the values system of an agrarian society contained in Nazi ideology and — above all — to legitimate this agrarian model and give Nazi policy a goal that was clearly oriented toward a far-reaching re-agrarianization.[39]

This goal was not only quite consonant with imperialist expansion in the name of *Lebensraum*, it was in fact one of its primary justifications, even motivations. In language replete with the biologistic metaphors of organicism, Darré declared:

"The concept of Blood and Soil gives us the moral right to take back as much land in the East as is necessary to establish a harmony between the body of our *Volk* and the geopolitical space."[40]

Aside from providing green camouflage for the colonization of Eastern Europe, Darré worked to install environmentally sensitive principles as the very basis of the Third Reich's agricultural policy. Even in its most productivist phases, these precepts remained emblematic of Nazi doctrine. When the "Battle for Production" (a scheme to boost the productivity of the agricultural sector) was proclaimed at the second Reich Farmers Congress in 1934, the very first point in the program read "Keep the soil healthy !" But Darré's most important innovation was the introduction on a large scale of organic farming methods, significantly labeled "lebensgesetzliche Landbauweise," or farming according to the laws of life. The term points up yet again the natural order ideology which underlies so much reactionary ecological thought. The impetus for these unprecedented measures came from Rudolf Steiner's anthroposophy and its techniques of biodynamic cultivation.[41]

The campaign to institutionalize organic farming encompassed tens of thousands of smallholdings and estates across Germany. It met with considerable resistance from other members of the Nazi hierarchy, above all Backe and Göring. But Darré, with the help of Hess and others, was able to sustain the policy until his forced resignation in 1942 (an event which had little to do with his environmentalist leanings). And these efforts in no sense represented merely Darré's personal predilections; as the standard history of German agricultural policy points out, Hitler and Himmler "were in complete sympathy with these ideas."[42] Still, it was largely Darré's influence in the Nazi apparatus which yielded, in practice, a level of government support for ecologically sound farming methods and land use planning unmatched by any state before or since.

For these reasons Darré has sometimes been regarded as a forerunner of the contemporary Green movement. His biographer, in fact, once referred to him as the "father of the Greens."[43] Her book *Blood and Soil*, undoubtedly the best single source on Darré in either German or English, consistently downplays the virulently fascist elements in his thinking, portraying him instead as a misguided agrarian radical. This grave error in judgement indicates the powerfully disorienting pull of an 'ecological' aura. Darré's published writings alone, dating back to the early twenties, are enough to indict him as a rabidly racist and jingoist ideologue particularly prone to a vulgar and hateful antisemitism (he spoke of Jews, revealingly, as "weeds"). His decade-long tenure as a loyal servant and, moreover, architect of the Nazi state demonstrates his dedication to Hitler's deranged cause. One account even claims that it was Darré who convinced Hitler and Himmler of the necessity of exterminating the Jews and Slavs.[44] The ecological aspects of his thought cannot, in sum, be separated from their thoroughly Nazi framework. Far from embodying the 'redeeming' facets of National Socialism, Darré represents the baleful specter of ecofascism in power.

IMPLEMENTING THE ECOFASCIST PROGRAM

It is frequently pointed out that the agrarian and romantic moments in Nazi ideology and policy were in constant tension with, if not in flat contradiction to, the technocratic-industrialist thrust of the Third Reich's rapid modernization. What is not often remarked is that even these modernizing tendencies had a significant ecological component. The two men principally responsible for sustaining this environmentalist commitment in the midst of intensive industrialization were *Reichsminister* Fritz Todt and his aide, the high-level planner and engineer Alwin Seifert.

Todt was "one of the most influential National Socialists,"[45] directly responsible for questions of technological and industrial policy. At his death in 1942 he headed three different cabinet-level ministries in addition to the enormous quasi-official *Organisation Todt*, and had "gathered the major technical tasks of the Reich into his own hands."[46] According to his successor, Albert Speer, Todt "loved nature" and "repeatedly had serious run-ins with Bormann, protesting against his despoiling the landscape around Obersalzberg."[47] Another source calls him simply "an ecologist."[48] This reputation is based chiefly on Todt's efforts to make Autobahn construction — one

of the largest building enterprises undertaken in this century —
as environmentally sensitive as possible.

The pre-eminent historian of German engineering describes
this commitment thus: "Todt demanded of the completed work
of technology a harmony with nature and with the landscape,
thereby fulfilling modern ecological principles of engineering
as well as the 'organological' principles of his own era along
with their roots in *völkisch* ideology."[49] The ecological aspects of
this approach to construction went well beyond an emphasis on
harmonious adaptation to the natural surroundings for aes-
thetic reasons; Todt also established strict criteria for respecting
wetlands, forests and ecologically sensitive areas. But just as
with Arndt, Riehl and Darré, these environmentalist concerns
were inseparably bound to a *völkisch*-nationalist outlook. Todt
himself expressed this connection succinctly: "The fulfillment of
mere transportation purposes is not the final aim of German
highway construction. The German highway must be an expression of its surrounding landscape and an expression of the
German essence."[50]

Todt's chief advisor and collaborator on environmental
issues was his lieutenant Alwin Seifert, whom Todt reportedly
once called a "fanatical ecologist."[51] Seifert bore the official title
of Reich Advocate for the Landscape, but his nickname within
the party was "Mr. Mother Earth." The appellation was de-
served; Seifert dreamed of a "total conversion from technology
to nature,"[52] and would often wax lyrical about the wonders of
German nature and the tragedy of "humankind's" carelessness.
As early as 1934 he wrote to Hess demanding attention to water
issues and invoking "work methods that are more attuned to
nature."[53] In discharging his official duties Seifert stressed the
importance of wilderness and energetically opposed monoculture, wetlands drainage and chemicalized agriculture. He criticized Darré as too moderate, and "called for an agricultural
revolution towards 'a more peasant-like, natural, simple' method
of farming, 'independent of capital'."[54]

With the Third Reich's technological policy entrusted to
figures such as these, even the Nazis' massive industrial build-
up took on a distinctively green hue. The prominence of nature
in the party's philosophical background helped ensure that

more radical initiatives often received a sympathetic hearing in the highest offices of the Nazi state. In the mid-thirties Todt and Seifert vigorously pushed for an all-encompassing Reich Law for the Protection of Mother Earth "in order to stem the steady loss of this irreplaceable basis of all life."[55] Seifert reports that all of the ministries were prepared to co-operate save one; only the minister of the economy opposed the bill because of its impact on mining.

But even near-misses such as these would have been unthinkable without the support of Reich Chancellor Rudolf Hess, who provided the "green wing" of the NSDAP a secure anchor at the very top of the party hierarchy. It would be difficult to overestimate Hess's power and centrality in the complex governmental machinery of the National Socialist regime. He joined the party in 1920 as member #16, and for two decades was Hitler's devoted personal deputy. He has been described as "Hitler's closest confidant,"[56] and the *Führer* himself referred to Hess as his "closest advisor."[57] Hess was not only the highest party leader and second in line (after Göring) to succeed Hitler; in addition, all legislation and every decree had to pass through his office before becoming law.

An inveterate nature lover as well as a devout Steinerite, Hess insisted on a strictly biodynamic diet — not even Hitler's rigorous vegetarian standards were good enough for him — and accepted only homeopathic medicines. It was Hess who introduced Darré to Hitler, thus securing the "green wing" its first power base. He was an even more tenacious proponent of organic farming than Darré, and pushed the latter to take more demonstrative steps in support of the *lebensgesetzliche Landbauweise*.[58] His office was also directly responsible for land use planning across the Reich, employing a number of specialists who shared Seifert's ecological approach.[59]

With Hess's enthusiastic backing, the "green wing" was able to achieve its most notable successes. As early as March 1933, a wide array of environmentalist legislation was approved and implemented at national, regional and local levels. These measures, which included reforestation programs, bills protecting animal and plant species, and preservationist decrees blocking industrial development, undoubtedly "ranked among the most progressive in the world at that time."[60] Planning ordinances were designed for the protection of wildlife habitat and at the same time demanded respect for the sacred German forest. The Nazi state also created the first nature preserves in Europe.

Along with Darré's efforts toward re-agrarianization and support for organic agriculture, as well as Todt and Seifert's attempts to institutionalize an environmentally sensitive land use planning and industrial policy, the major accomplishment of the Nazi ecologists was the *Reichsnaturschutzgesetz* of 1935. This completely unprecedented "nature protection law" not only established guidelines for safeguarding flora, fauna, and "natural monuments" across the Reich; it also restricted commercial access to remaining tracts of wilderness. In addition, the comprehensive ordinance "required all national, state and local officials to consult with Naturschutz authorities in a timely manner before undertaking any measures that would produce fundamental alterations in the countryside."[61]

Although the legislation's effectiveness was questionable, traditional German environmentalists were overjoyed at its passage. Walter Schoenichen declared it the "definitive fulfillment of the *völkisch*-romantic longings,"[62] and Hans Klose, Schoenichen's successor as head of the Reich Agency for Nature Protection, described Nazi environmental policy as the "high point of nature protection" in Germany. Perhaps the greatest success of these measures was in facilitating the "intellectual realignment of German Naturschutz" and the integration of mainstream environmentalism into the Nazi enterprise.[63]

While the achievements of the "green wing" were daunting, they should not be exaggerated. Ecological initiatives were, of course, hardly universally popular within the party. Goebbels, Bormann, and Heydrich, for example, were implacably opposed to them, and considered Darré, Hess and their fellows undependable dreamers, eccentrics, or simply security risks. This latter suspicion seemed to be confirmed by Hess's famed flight to Britain in 1941; after that point, the environmentalist tendency was for the most part suppressed. Todt was killed in a plane crash in February 1942, and shortly thereafter Darré was stripped of all his posts. For the final three years of the Nazi conflagration the "green wing" played no active role. Their work, however, had long since left an indelible stain.

Fascist Ecology in Context

To make this dismaying and discomforting analysis more palatable, it is tempting to draw precisely the wrong conclusion — namely, that even the most reprehensible political undertakings sometimes produce laudable results. But the real lesson here is just the opposite: Even the most laudable of causes can be perverted and instrumentalized in the service of criminal savagery. The "green wing" of the NSDAP was not a group of innocents, confused and manipulated idealists, or reformers from within; they were conscious promoters and executors of a vile program explicitly dedicated to inhuman racist violence, massive political repression and worldwide military domination. Their 'ecological' involvements, far from offsetting these fundamental commitments, deepened and radicalized them. In the end, their configuration of environmental politics was directly and substantially responsible for organized mass murder.

No aspect of the Nazi project can be properly understood without examining its implication in the holocaust. Here, too, ecological arguments played a crucially malevolent role. Not only did the "green wing" refurbish the sanguine antisemitism of traditional reactionary ecology; it catalyzed a whole new outburst of lurid racist fantasies of organic inviolability and political revenge. The confluence of anti-humanist dogma with a fetishization of natural 'purity' provided not merely a rationale but an incentive for the Third Reich's most heinous crimes. Its insidious appeal unleashed murderous energies previously untapped. Finally, the displacement of any social analysis of environmental destruction in favor of mystical ecology served as an integral component in the preparation of the final solution:

> To explain the destruction of the countryside and environmental damage, without questioning the German people's bond to nature, could only be done by not analysing environmental damage in a societal context and by refusing to understand them as an expression of

conflicting social interests. Had this been done, it would have led to criticism of National Socialism itself since that was not immune to such forces. One solution was to associate such environmental problems with the destructive influence of other races. National Socialism could then be seen to strive for the elimination of other races in order to allow the German people's innate understanding and feeling of nature to assert itself, hence securing a harmonic life close to nature for the future.[64]

This is the true legacy of ecofascism in power: "genocide developed into a necessity under the cloak of environment protection."[65]

* * *

The experience of the "green wing" of German fascism is a sobering reminder of the political volatility of ecology. It certainly does not indicate any inherent or inevitable connection between ecological issues and right-wing politics; alongside the reactionary tradition surveyed here, there has always been an equally vital heritage of left-libertarian ecology, in Germany as elsewhere.[66] But certain patterns can be discerned: "While concerns about problems posed by humankind's increasing mastery over nature have increasingly been shared by ever larger groups of people embracing a plethora of ideologies, the most consistent 'pro-natural order' response found political embodiment on the radical right."[67] This is the common thread which unites merely conservative or even supposedly apolitical manifestations of environmentalism with the straightforwardly fascist variety.

The historical record does, to be sure, belie the vacuous claim that "those who want to reform society according to nature are neither left nor right but ecologically minded."[68] Environmental themes can be mobilized from the left or from the right, indeed they *require* an explicit social context if they are to have any political valence whatsoever. "Ecology" alone does not prescribe a politics; it must be interpreted, mediated through some theory of society in order to acquire political meaning. Failure to heed this mediated interrelationship between the social and the ecological is the hallmark of reactionary ecology.

As noted above, this failure most commonly takes the form of a call to "reform society according to nature," that is, to formulate some version of 'natural order' or 'natural law' and submit human needs and actions to it. As a consequence, the underlying social processes and societal structures which constitute and shape people's relations with their environment are left unexamined. Such willful ignorance, in turn, obscures the ways in which all conceptions of nature are themselves socially produced, and leaves power structures unquestioned while simultaneously providing them with apparently 'naturally ordained' status. Thus the substitution of ecomysticism for clearsighted social-ecological inquiry has catastrophic political repercussions, as the complexity of the society-nature dialectic is collapsed into a purified Oneness. An ideologically charged 'natural order' does not leave room for compromise; its claims are absolute.

For all of these reasons, the slogan advanced by many contemporary Greens, "We are neither right nor left but up front," is historically naive and politically fatal. The necessary project of creating an emancipatory ecological politics demands an acute awareness and understanding of the legacy of classical ecofascism and its conceptual continuities with present-day environmental discourse. An 'ecological' orientation alone, outside of a critical social framework, is dangerously unstable. The record of fascist ecology shows that under the right conditions such an orientation can quickly lead to barbarism.

FOOTNOTES

1. Ernst Lehmann, *Biologischer Wille. Wege und Ziele biologischer Arbeit im neuen Reich*, München, 1934, pp. 10-11. Lehmann was a professor of botany who characterized National Socialism as "politically applied biology."

2. Anna Bramwell, author of the only book-length study on the subject, is exemplary in this respect. See her *Blood and Soil: Walther Darré and Hitler's 'Green Party'*, Bourne End, 1985, and *Ecology in the 20th Century: A History*, New Haven, 1989.

3. See Raymond H. Dominick, *The Environmental Movement in Germany: Prophets and Pioneers, 1871-1971*, Bloomington, 1992, especially part three, "The Völkisch Temptation."

4. For example, Dominick, *The Environmental Movement in Germany*, p. 22; and Jost Hermand, *Grüne Utopien in Deutschland: Zur Geschichte des ökologischen Bewußtseins*, Frankfurt, 1991, pp. 44-45.

5. Quoted in Rudolf Krügel, *Der Begriff des Volksgeistes in Ernst Moritz Arndts Geschichtsanschauung*, Langensalza, 1914, p. 18.

6. Wilhelm Heinrich Riehl, *Feld und Wald*, Stuttgart, 1857, p. 52.

7. Klaus Bergmann, *Agrarromantik und Großstadtfeindschaft*, Meisenheim, 1970, p. 38. There is no satisfactory English counterpart to "Großstadtfeindschaft," a term which signifies hostility to the cosmopolitanism, internationalism, and cultural tolerance of cities as such. This 'anti-urbanism' is the precise opposite of the careful critique of urbanization worked out by Murray Bookchin in *Urbanization Without Cities*, Montréal, 1992, and *The Limits of the City*, Montréal, 1986.

8. George Mosse, *The Crisis of German Ideology: Intellectual Origins of the Third Reich*, New York, 1964, p. 29.

9. Lucy Dawidowicz, *The War Against the Jews 1933-1945*, New York, 1975, pp. 61-62.

10. Daniel Gasman, *The Scientific Origins of National Socialism: Social Darwinism in Ernst Haeckel and the German Monist League*, New York, 1971, p. xvii.

11. ibid., p. 30. Gasman's thesis about the politics of Monism is hardly uncontroversial; the book's central argument, however, is sound.

12. Quoted in Gasman, *The Scientific Origins of National Socialism*, p. 34.

13. ibid., p. 33.

14. See the foreword to the 1982 reprint of his 1923 book *Die Entdeckung der Heimat*, published by the far-right MUT Verlag.

15. Mosse, *The Crisis of German Ideology*, p. 101.

16. Walter Laqueur, *Young Germany: A History of the German Youth Movement*, New York, 1962, p.41.

17. ibid., p. 6. For a concise portrait of the youth movement which draws similiar conclusions, see John De Graaf, "The Wandervogel," *CoEvolution Quarterly*, Fall 1977, pp. 14-21.

18. Reprinted in Ludwig Klages, *Sämtliche Werke*, Band 3, Bonn, 1974, pp. 614-630. No English translation is available.

19. Ulrich Linse, *Ökopax und Anarchie. Eine Geschichte der ökologischen Bewegungen in Deutschland*, München, 1986, p. 60.

20. Mosse, *The Crisis of German Ideology*, p. 211, and Laqueur, *Young Germany*, p. 34.

21. See Fritz Stern, *The Politics of Cultural Despair*, Berkeley, 1963.

22. Michael Zimmerman, *Heidegger's Confrontation with Modernity: Technology, Politics and Art*, Indianapolis, 1990, pp. 242-243.

23. See Michael Zimmerman, "Rethinking the Heidegger — Deep Ecology Relationship", *Environmental Ethics* vol. 15, no. 3 (Fall 1993), pp. 195-224.

24. Reproduced in Joachim Wolschke-Bulmahn, *Auf der Suche nach Arkadien*, München, 1990, p. 147.

25. Robert Pois, *National Socialism and the Religion of Nature*, London, 1985, p. 40.

26. ibid., pp. 42-43. The internal quote is taken from George Mosse, *Nazi Culture*, New York, 1965, p. 87.

27. Hitler, in Henry Picker, *Hitlers Tischgespräche im Führerhauptquartier 1941-1942*, Stuttgart, 1963, p. 151.

28. Adolf Hitler, *Mein Kampf*, München, 1935, p. 314.

29. Quoted in Gert Gröning and Joachim Wolschke-Bulmahn, "Politics, planning and the protection of nature: political abuse of early ecological ideas in Germany, 1933-1945", *Planning Perspectives* 2 (1987), p. 129.

30. Änne Bäumer, *NS-Biologie*, Stuttgart, 1990, p. 198.

31. Alfred Rosenberg, *Der Mythus des 20. Jahrhunderts*, München, 1938, p. 550. Rosenberg was, in the early years at least, the chief ideologist of the Nazi movement.

32. Picker, *Hitlers Tischgespräche*, pp. 139-140.

33. Quoted in Heinz Haushofer, *Ideengeschichte der Agrarwirtschaft und Agrarpolitik im deutschen Sprachgebiet*, Band II, München, 1958, p. 266.

34. See Dominick, *The Environmental Movement in Germany*, p. 107.

35. ibid., p. 113.

36. Bergmann, *Agrarromantik und Großstadtfeindschaft*, p. 334. Ernst Nolte makes a similar argument in *Three Faces of Fascism*, New York, 1966, pp. 407-408, though the point gets lost somewhat in the translation. See also Norbert Frei, *National Socialist Rule in Germany*, Oxford, 1993, p. 56: "The change in direction towards the 'soil' had not been an electoral tactic. It was one of the basic ideological elements of National Socialism . . . "

37. R. Walther Darré, *Um Blut und Boden: Reden und Aufsätze*, München, 1939, p. 28. The quote is from a 1930 speech entitled "Blood and Soil as the Foundations of Life of the Nordic Race."

38. Bramwell, *Ecology in the 20th Century*, p. 203. See also Frei, *National Socialist Rule in Germany*, p. 57, which stresses that Darré's total control over agricultural policy constituted a uniquely powerful position within the Nazi system.

39. Bergmann, *Agrarromantik und Großstadtfeindschaft*, p. 312.

40. ibid., p. 308.

41. See Haushofer, *Ideengeschichte der Agrarwirtschaft*, pp. 269-271, and Bramwell, *Ecology in the 20th Century*, pp. 200-206, for the formative influence of Steinerite ideas on Darré.

42. Haushofer, *Ideengeschichte der Agrarwirtschaft*, p. 271.

43. Anna Bramwell, "Darré. Was This Man 'Father of the Greens'?" *History Today*, September 1984, vol. 34, pp. 7-13. This repugnant article is one long series of distortions designed to paint Darré as an anti-Hitler hero — an effort as preposterous as it is loathsome.

44. Roger Manvell and Heinrich Fraenkel, *Hess: A Biography*, London, 1971, p. 34.

45. Franz Neumann, *Behemoth. The Structure and Practice of National Socialism 1933-1944*, New York, 1944, p. 378.

46. Albert Speer, *Inside the Third Reich*, New York, 1970, p. 263.

47. ibid., p. 261.

48. Bramwell, *Ecology in the 20th Century*, p. 197.

49. Karl-Heinz Ludwig, *Technik und Ingenieure im Dritten Reich*, Düsseldorf, 1974, p. 337.

50. Quoted in Rolf Peter Sieferle, *Fortschrittsfeinde? Opposition gegen Technik und Industrie von der Romantik bis zur Gegenwart*, München, 1984, p. 220. Todt was just as convinced a Nazi as Darré or Hess; on the extent (and pettiness) of his allegiance to antisemitic policies, see Alan Beyerchen, *Scientists Under Hitler*, New Haven, 1977, pages 66-68 and 289.

51. Bramwell, *Blood and Soil*, p. 173.

52. Alwin Seifert, *Im Zeitalter des Lebendigen*, Dresden, 1941, p. 13. The book's title is grotesquely inapt considering the date of publication; it means "in the age of the living."

53. Alwin Seifert, *Ein Leben für die Landschaft*, Düsseldorf, 1962, p. 100.

54. Bramwell, *Ecology in the 20th Century*, p. 198. Bramwell cites Darré's papers as the source of the internal quote.

55. Seifert, *Ein Leben für die Landschaft*, p. 90.

56. William Shirer, *Berlin Diary*, New York, 1941, p. 19. Shirer also calls Hess Hitler's "protégé" (588) and "the only man in the world he fully trusts" (587), and substantiates Darré's and Todt's standing as well (590).

57. Quoted in Manvell and Fraenkel, *Hess*, p. 80. In a further remarkable confirmation of the 'green' faction's stature, Hitler once declared that Todt and Hess were "the only two human beings among all those around me to whom I have been truly and inwardly attached" (*Hess*, p. 132).

58. See Haushofer, *Ideengeschichte der Agrarwirtschaft*, p. 270, and Bramwell, *Ecology in the 20th Century*, p. 201.

59. ibid., pp. 197-200. Most of Todt's work also ran through Hess's office.

60. Raymond Dominick, "The Nazis and the Nature Conservationists", *The Historian* vol. XLIX no. 4 (August 1987), p. 534.

61. ibid., p. 536.

62. Hermand, *Grüne Utopien in Deutschland*, p. 114.

63. Dominick, "The Nazis and the Nature Conservationists", p. 529.

64. Gröning and Wolschke-Bulmahn, "Politics, planning and the protection of nature", p. 137.

65. ibid., p. 138.

66. Linse's *Ökopax und Anarchie*, among others, offers a detailed consideration of the history of eco-anarchism in Germany.

67. Pois, *National Socialism and the Religion of Nature*, p. 27.

68. Bramwell, *Ecology in the 20th Century*, p. 48.

'Ecology' and the Modernization of Fascism in the German Ultra-right

Janet Biehl

It is an incontestable fact that the ecology crisis today is real. In a vast number of ways and places, the biosphere of this planet is undergoing a great deal of damage. Parts of the environment have already been rendered uninhabitable through toxic wastes and nuclear power plant disasters, while systemic pollution, ozone holes, global warming, and other disasters are increasingly tearing the fabric on which all life depends. That such damage is wrought overwhelmingly by corporations in a competitive international market economy has never been clearer, while the need to replace the existing society with one such as social ecology advances has never been more urgent.[1]

At a time when worsening economic conditions and strong political disaffection occur along with ecological dislocations, however, nationalist and even fascist ideas are gaining an increasingly high profile in Europe, particularly, but not only, in the Federal Republic of Germany. With social tensions exacerbated, neofascist groups of various kinds are winning electoral representation, even as their loosely linked cohorts commit acts of violence against foreigners. Such groups, both skinhead and 'intellectual,' are part of a 'New' Right that explicitly draws its

This article was originally published in *Society and Nature: The International Journal of Political Ecology*, vol. 2, no. 2 (1994).

ideas from classical fascism. They are updating the old nationalist, mystical, and misanthropic themes of the 'Old' Right,
writes Jutta Ditfurth, in a "modernization of fascism." Among
other things, they are using a right-wing interpretation of
ecology "as an ideological 'hinge' for organizing the extreme-
right and neofascist scene." [2]

Today's fascists have a distinct ideological legacy from
their fascist forebears upon which to draw. Indeed, 'ecology'
and a mystical reverence for the natural world are hardly new
to German nationalism. At the end of the nineteenth century, a
cultural revolt against positivism swept much of Europe, as
George L. Mosse writes, and in Germany it became infused with
both nature-mysticism and racial nationalism. This revolt

> became intimately bound up with a belief in nature's
> cosmic life force, a dark force whose mysteries could be
> understood, not through science, but through the oc-
> cult. An ideology based upon such premises was fused
> with the glories of an Aryan past, and in turn, that past
> received a thoroughly romantic and mystical
> interpretation.[3]

Culminating in the 1920s, an assortment of occult and pseudo-
scientific ideas coalesced around the idea of a German *Volk* into
a romantic nationalism, romantic racism, and a mystical na-
ture-worshipping faith. Indeed, as Mosse observes, the German
word *Volk*

> is a much more comprehensive term than "people," for
> to German thinkers ever since the birth of German
> romanticism in the late eighteenth century "Volk" sig-
> nified the union of a group of people with a transcen-
> dental "essence." This "essence" might be called "na-
> ture" or "cosmos" or "mythos," but in each instance it
> was fused to man's innermost nature, and represented
> the source of his creativity, his depth of feeling, his
> individuality, and his unity with other members of the
> Volk.[4]

The *völkisch* movement of the 1920s regarded modern materialism, urbanism, rationalism, and science as artificial and evil, alien to this 'essence.'[5] In a time of bitter social dislocation, it saw Weimar democracy as the product of Western democratic and liberal ideals and, further, as a puppet regime controlled by people who did not represent German 'essence.' Many alleged that a Jewish world conspiracy lay behind the discontents of modernism, including materialistic consumerism, soulless industrialism, a homogenized commercial culture, and excessive modern technology, all of which were said to be systematically destroying traditional German values. Only true patriots could save Germans from ruin, thought the extreme right — themselves.

This movement sought to assert a truly Germanic alternative — one as racialist as it was nationalist in nature. The popular writings of Paul Lagarde and Julius Langbehn favored an aristocratic social order in which Germans would rule the world. It invoked a nature-romanticism in which a closeness to the natural landscape was to give people a heightened sense of aliveness and 'authenticity.' It advanced a new cosmic faith, embodied in 'Aryan' blood, that was to be grasped through intuition rather than science in a plethora of occult and esoteric spiritualistic faiths that abounded in Germany in the 1920s. Mystical belief-systems like Theosophy, Anthroposophy, and Ariosophy (a mystical Aryanism) abounded and were rife with Germanic-nationalist components, such that they could be used to mystify an 'ecological' nationalism.

However inadvertently, the romantic nationalists of the *völkisch* movement became an important source for National Socialist ideology, which ironically drew on its antimodern sentiments even as it built a technologically modern and virulently nationalistic and genocidal totalitarian state. Demagogically appealing to a very real sense of alienation, the Nazis stage-managed indoctrination extravaganzas that promised 'authenticity' in a mystical, romantic nationalism that was 'closer to nature,' even as they engaged in mass murder. Stressing the need to return to simpler, healthier, and more 'natural' lifeways, they advanced the idea and practice of a 'Nordic peasantry' tied organically to the soil — even as they constructed a society that was industrially more modernized and rationalized than any German society had seen to that time.

The so-called 'New' Right today appeals to themes reminiscent of the *völkisch* movement in pre-Nazi Germany. It, too, presents itself as offering an 'ecological' alternative to modern society. In the view of the 'New' Right today, the destruction of the environment and the repression of nationalities have a common root in 'Semitic' monotheism and universalism. In its later form, Christianity, and in its subsequent secularized forms, liberalism and Marxism, this dualistic, homogenizing universalism is alleged to have brought on both the ecological crisis and the suppression of national identity. Just as Judeo-Christian universalism was destructive of authentic cultures when Christian missionaries went out into the world, so too is modernity eliminating ethnic and national cultures. Moreover, through the unbridled technology to which it gave rise, this modern universalism is said to have perpetrated not only the destruction of nature but an annihilation of the spirit; the destruction of nature, it is said, is life-threatening in the spiritual sense as well as the physical, since when people deny pristine nature, their access to their 'authentic' self is blocked.

The dualistic yet universalistic 'Semitic' legacy is borne today most egregiously, in 'New' Right ideology, by the United States, in whose 'mongrel' culture — egalitarian democracy — all cultures and races are mixed together, forming a crass, soulless society. American cultural imperialism is genocidal of other cultures around the world, and its technological imperialism is destroying the global environment. The fascist quest for 'national identity' and ecological salvation seeks to counter 'Western civilization' — that is, the United States, as opposed to 'European civilization' — by advancing a notion of 'ethnopluralism' that seeks for all cultures to have sovereignty over themselves and their environment. Europe should become, instead of a modernized monoculture, a 'Europe of fatherlands,' with autonomy for all its peoples. Just as Turks should live in Turkey and Senegalese in Senegal, Germans should have Germany for themselves, 'New' Right ideologues argue.

Ecology can easily be perverted to justify this 'ethnopluralism' — that is, nationalism. Conceptions of one's region as one's 'homeland,' or *Heimat*, can be perverted into a nationalistic regionalism when a region's traditions and language are mystically tied to an 'ancestral' landscape. (The word *Heimat* connotes as well a turn toward the past, an anti-urban mood, a familiar community, and proximity to nature. For several decades the concept was looked upon with disfavor because the Nazis had used it, but intellectuals rediscovered it in the 1970s, after further decades of capitalist industrialization.) For a people seeking to assert themselves against an outside intruder, an 'ecologized' *Heimat* in which they are biologically embedded can become a useful tool not only against imperialism but against immigration, foreigners, and 'overpopulation.' Elaborate justifications for opposing Third World immigration are disguised as diversity, drawing on 'ecological' arguments against 'overpopulation.' Today it is not only fascists who invoke *Heimat*; in September 1989, for example, the head of the respectable League for the Protection of the Environment and Nature (Bund für Umwelt- und Naturschutz, or BUND), environmentalist Hubert Weinzierl, remarked that

> only when humanity's main concern, the diminution of the stream of overpopulation, has been accomplished, will there be any meaning or any prospect of building an environment that is capable of improvement, of configuring the landscape of our civilization in such a way that it remains worthy of being called *Heimat*. [6]

An ecology that is mystical, in turn, may become a justification for a nationalism that is mystical. In the New Age milieu of today, with its affinities for ecology, the ultra-right may well find the mystical component it needs to make a truly updated, modernized authoritarian nationalism. As in Germany between the two world wars, antirational cults of the New Age — primitivistic, esoteric — abound in both the Federal Republic and the Anglo-American world. Such antirationalism and mysticism are appealed to by the 'New' Right; as anarchist publisher Wolfgang Haug observes, "The New Right, in effect, wants above all to redefine social norms so that rational doubt is regarded as decadent and eliminated, and new 'natural' norms are established."[7]

Neofascist 'Ecology'

Ecology is warped for mystical-nationalist ends by a whole series of neofascist groups and parties. Indeed, so multifarious are the ecofascist parties that have arisen, and so much do their memberships overlap, that they form what antifascist researcher Volkmar Wölk calls an "ecofascist network."[8] Their programmatic literature often combines ecology and nationalism in ways that are designed to appeal to people who do not consider themselves fascists, while at the same time they ideologically support neo-Nazi street-fighting skinheads who commit acts of violence against foreigners.

National Revolutionaries[9]

The National Revolutionaries (NRs) manipulatively mix themes of left and right in their uses of nationalism and ecology, in an attempt to cross ideological lines. They draw on an old tenet of right-wing dissent in Germany — the belief that a 'Third Way' between capitalism and socialism is necessary and that Germany is predestined to lead humankind toward it.[10] The NRs' 'Third Way' is based on nationalism, a socialism "of the specific national way" [11] — in short, a 'national socialism.' A wing of the NRs today, called the Solidaristen, identifies itself with the Strasser brothers, two 1920s Nazi Party members who took the 'Socialism' in 'National Socialism' seriously and represented the 'left' anticapitalist wing of the Nazis. Today, the Solidaristen and other NRs regard Otto Strasser in particular as the 'Trotsky of National Socialism' because of his 1920s intraparty power struggle with Hitler; Hitler's ejection of this fascist in 1930 was, for them, a betrayal of National Socialism.

Today's leading NR ideologist, Henning Eichberg, calls for the assertion of "national identity" and a "liberation nationalism." Seeking to appeal to left and right, NR publications have supported national liberation movements from across the traditional political spectrum, including the Irish, Basques, Ukrainians, and Afghans, as well as Sandinistas.[12] They regarded divided Germany as an occupied country, "the result of the imperialist politics of the occupation forces," and they sought to "liberate" it — including Austria. Now that Germany has been freed from this "occupation," the National Revolutionaries are free to concentrate on "reunifying" with Austria.

Eichberg regards Judeo-Christianity as the ultimate root of all present evils, since it is overly intellectual and alienates humanity both from itself and from the divine; it neglects the emotions and the body. Tied in as it is with the logic of productivism, Christianity, Eichberg writes, is the "religion of growth" that must be fought at all costs. To help cultivate 'national identity,' he proposes instead a new religion that mixes together neopagan Germanic, Celtic, and Indian religions with old *völkisch*-nationalistic ideas. It is to be based on "the sensuality-physicality of dance and ritual, ceremony and taboo, meditation, prayer, and ecstasy. In essence, [this religion] constitutes itself as a form of praxis" against the "religion of growth" since its "sensuous counter-experiences" can restore humanity to closer contact with nature. Sounding like many New Agers in the United States, Eichberg calls for a return to pristine nature, to the alleged primordial sources of people's lives, psyches, and authentic cultures, and for people to heal themselves within as part of healing the ecological crisis, overcoming their own alienation, and rediscovering themselves.[13]

National Revolutionaries exploit ecological themes not only to construct primitivistic New Age religions but for political activity as well. During the 1970s they organized around opposition to nuclear energy at about the same time as the citizens' initiative movement did. "With their ecological and antinuclear enthusiasm," observes Walter Laqueur,

> their cultural anti-Americanism and their support for movements of national liberation in many parts of the world, the "national revolutionaries" tried, in fact, to outflank their left-wing contemporaries. Some regarded Sinn Fein as a model for the German national revolutionaries, others suggested "political Balkanization" in

Germany and Europe as a solution to all outstanding questions.[14]

Other National Revolutionaries took a different political approach: at the end of the 1970s, they joined the newly emerging Greens, where some of their number succeeded in holding office for a time. In October 1980, the Alternative List of West Berlin, for one, decided they could not work with National Revolutionaries, whom they considered even more dangerous than overt neo-Nazis because they hid their true intentions behind a veil of grassroots democratic and ecological programs. They were mostly driven out of the Greens, at least as far as observers seem aware today.[15]

The Freedom German Workers Party [16]

Like the National Revolutionaries, the Freedom German Workers Party (Freiheitliche Deutsche Arbeiterpartei, or FAP) calls for a 'national socialism,' albeit one based on "a sense of community instead of class struggle." The FAP seeks no rapprochement with leftists; it openly and militantly proclaims its support for Nazi ideas, celebrates race and nation, and is pro-Hitler rather than Strasserite. It praises German soldiers, whose "achievements" in two world wars will "still be admired in a thousand years." The FAP is largely controlled by The Movement (Die Bewegung), which seeks to reestablish the NSDAP (the Nazi Party) in the Federal Republic and unite all fascist groups under its aegis.[17]

The FAP recruits from among skinheads and soccer fans, and its activities include acts of violence, arson, and racial attacks on foreigners. It advances the crudest 'Germany for Germans — foreigners out' slogans.[18] When it engages in electoral activity, its programmatic demands have included "German jobs for German workers," "repatriation for foreigners," "no franchise for foreigners," and an end to the "crazy enthusiasm for integration."[19] Germans today must not ruin the "legacy of our fathers," the "cultural landscape"; Alsace-Lorraine, the South Tyrol, and Austria should all be returned to Germany.

FAP Nazis especially loathe "humanistically oriented cosmopolitanism." Marxism, liberalism, and Christianity "have torn humanity from its connectedness to the natural cycles of our earth." No "technical environmentalism" will succeed against the "increasingly obvious ecological catastrophe," they believe. Rather, the "disrupted relations between humanity and the rest of nature" require an "ecological revolution" and a "radical revolution in consciousness" that will "lead humanity to a reintegration with the structure of planetary life." We need a new ethics, they maintain, one in which "humanity, animals and nature are regarded as a unity. Animals are not things" but are "life-forms that feel joy and pain and need our protection." Not surprisingly, the FAP regards abortion as a "crime against the laws of a healthy nature and against God."

In a blatant self-contradiction, their concrete environmental demands are in fact friendly to capitalism: They want "continued economic growth," yet less profit-seeking. "Ecological necessities . . . must be brought into accordance with a functioning economy," they believe, while "the cyclical system of nature should . . . be incorporated into the economic realm."

The Republicans [20]

The Republicans, a political party founded by former Waffen-SS member Franz Schönhuber in 1983, have made numerous disavowals of any association with the Nazis — they present themselves as nothing more than a "community of German patriots." Yet this does not stop them from taking explicitly anti-immigrant stances, especially against Turks, or from exploiting discontents about the influx of foreigners generally, or from maintaining that Germany should be "for Germans." The presence of a "tidal wave" of asylum-seekers in the Federal Republic, they believe, causes "the importation of criminals," "social tensions," and "financial burdens."

The Republicans call for the "preservation of the existence of the German *Volk*, its health and its ecological living-space [*Lebensraum*] as a priority for domestic policy. This goal," they add, "will also foster environmental protection." Indeed, ecological dislocations are endangering Germans' "health" — and by 'health' they mean the 'genetic health' of the German people. Such 'health' has "a higher value than short-term profits and striving for a standard of living." Protecting and maintaining a "healthy environment" not only assures the "security of the means of life of our people" but is "a patriotic duty." The Republicans are stringently antiabortion for German women, yet for the Third World, "meaningful family planning" is necessary to end the "population explosion" and its consequent threat to the environment; without it there will be "natural catastrophe and starvation."

The National Democratic Party [21]

The National Democratic Party of Germany (National-demokratische Partei Deutschlands, or NPD), founded in 1964 mainly by people who had been active Nazis before 1945, rose to prominence during the 1960s. This aggressively nationalist party long called for German reunification, while its programmatic literature complains that "two wars within one generation . . . have eaten away at the substantive health of the German people." (It does not mention what those wars did to the Jews, as Ditfurth dryly notes.) The NPD laments the destruction of the environment, which "has disadvantageous effects on the *Volk*-health." Germans should not be exposed to "chemical dyes" and should be protected from "congenital illness," while people with AIDS should be required to "register." The "preservation" of the "German people" requires that German women prolifically give birth, and therefore the NPD is against the "devaluation and destruction of the family." Since abortion threatens "the biological existence of our people," women who have abortions should be punished. The party calls for maternal and housekeeping training for "feminine youth."

In 1973, the NPD drew up an "Ecological Manifesto" that invoked "the laws of nature" to justify a hierarchically structured, "organic" order that would govern social relationships.[22] It inveighs against "the environment polluted and poisoned by a humanity that lives increasingly isolated in a degraded mass," which "is only the most noticeable symptom of the ruined equilibrium of humanity and nature." In the years since then, the NPD's rhetoric has become increasingly New Age oriented; it now calls for "reachieving . . . an environmental consciousness, so necessary for life." Achieving this consciousness, the 1988 NPD program states, "first requires an inner revolution in human thought. It is not the unlimited accumulation of material goods or boundless consumption that gives meaning to human life and happiness, but the experience of nature, concern for cultural values, and social security in the family and *Volk*." Indeed, "*Volk*-consciousness and environmental consciousness are inseparable," since "millions of strangers" threaten "our *Volk* in its existence."

The German People's Union[23]

The German People's Union (Deutsche Volksunion, or DVU) was founded by Dr. Gerhard Frey (born in 1933), a longtime ultra-right activist and publisher. Still its leading figure, Frey has been fixated for decades on the Second World War in DVU publications, casting doubts on the concentration camps as they are normally depicted and generally denying German guilt; his publications offer Nazi memorabilia for sale. The DVU proclaims that "Germany should remain German" and calls for "priority in German housing for Germans" and "national identity and self-determination." For the DVU, environmental protection means passing "stringent laws against polluters," "strict examination of imported foodstuffs," and imposing restrictions on animal experimentation and on "the torture of animals." Protecting life means "an end to abortion abuse."

ANTHROPOSOPHY AND THE WORLD LEAGUE
FOR THE PROTECTION OF LIFE

Political parties like these have an assortment of 'Old' Right — that is, Nazi — connections upon which they may draw in their search for 'ecological' modernization. One such connection is the World League for the Protection of Life (Weltbund Schutz des Lebens, or WSL). This group is not without a certain general appeal in the Federal Republic, since its outlook is based on Anthroposophy, a body of occult ideas formulated earlier in this century by Rudolf Steiner (1861-1925). Steiner, the leading German figure in the nineteenth-century esoteric 'wisdom' cult Theosophy, founded the German Theosophical Society; he went on to found his own doctrine, Anthroposophy, and the Anthroposophical Society thereafter. He wrote many books on his occult spiritualistic philosophy.

Anthroposophy holds a particular attraction in the German counterculture today, as it did in the *völkisch* movement of the 1920s. The Waldorf Schools, for example, were founded on Steiner's educational principles and are respectable in many German and American countercultural circles. (There are more than sixty in the Federal Republic today.) Founded by Steiner in 1920, they provide children with an alternative, reformed education, one that is free from aggression and from pressures to achieve, one that places emphasis on the musical aspects of life and on feelings over understanding. Steiner is also the founder of biodynamic farming, a form of organic agriculture that does without pesticides and tries to foster a more organic relationship between cultivator and soil. Biodynamic agriculturists today produce a line of organic foods under the brand name Demeter and a line of cosmetics under the name Weleda. Many people have been and continue to be innocently attracted to these efforts and to Anthroposophy without any notion of the less savory aspects of Steiner's work.

Yet not all of Steiner's beliefs were benignly ecospiritual. For one thing, Anthroposophy classifies humanity into 'root races' in an esoteric evolutionary theory.[24] Building on a similar doctrine in Theosophy, the root-race theory is integral to Anthroposophy's cosmology. According to this doctrine, a series of root races of human beings evolved sequentially over the millennia, each superior to the ones that preceded it, each with a higher level of development of self-consciousness. The first two root races, the Polar and Hyperborean, were 'astral-etheric'; they are now extinct — the evolutionary process superseded them. The next people to evolve were a bit higher, but they were still half animal, purely instinctive, lacking the capacity for conceptual thought and memory. The fourth root race finally began to be recognizably human; finally came the Atlantans, to which Europeans belong. The European whites, as the most highly developed so far, are at the summit of the hierarchical scale of humanity; they have brought everything that is good to humanity, since they "are the only ones who have developed humanity within themselves."[25] These various races have been mostly killed off in various catastrophes of one kind or another, after which only certain people — presumably the fittest — survived; "in the case of the inferior kinds of human beings," wrote Steiner, "... the life body was not sufficiently protected to enable it to withstand the Luciferic influence."[26]

There are numerous subdivisions within these basic root races. Blacks, for example, must live in Africa, we learn, a land of much heat and light; blacks soak up this heat and light, and their brains are specially constructed to process it; their supposed highly instinctual nature results from all this processing.

And since the sun, light, and heat are retained in his epidermis, [the black's] whole metabolism proceeds as if he were being cooked inside himself by the sun. From this results his instinctive life. Within the black, he is continuously being cooked, and what stokes this fire is his posterior brain. [27]

Once blacks emigrate out of Africa, the balance of light and heat is different, and therefore they will die out — "they are in fact a declining race, they will die out of their own nature, since they are receiving too little light and heat."[28] Such a theory would justify accelerating the extinction of races since they are presumably going to die off anyway. In the future, wrote Steiner in 1909, certain people who have not reached a "high level of development" will incline toward evil: "The laggard souls will have accumulated in their karma so much error, ugliness, and evil that there will form, for the time being, a special union of evil and aberrant human beings who voluntarily oppose the community of good men." [29]

Perhaps this root-race theory was what appealed to Rudolf Hess about Anthroposophy, for he became an Anthroposophist. As Ditfurth points out, "The root-race ideology of the Theosophists and the Anthroposophists melded seamlessly into the National Socialist idea of the purity of the 'Aryan race.'"[30]

Certainly Steiner's ideas on biodynamic farming influenced some National Socialists. Anthroposophical ideas are eminently usable by ecofascists today, and there is a strong right wing within the Anthroposophists that is closely connected with the ultra-right. Author Günther Bartsch is an Anthroposophist who is also a National Revolutionary of the Solidarist variety; the author of an adulatory 1989 biography of Otto Strasser, he attempts in his publications to synthesize ecological themes based on Steiner's ideas with Strasser's political ideas.[31] It should be noted that Anthroposophy is also well funded by huge multinational corporations like Siemens and Bertelsmann. [32]

Among the ultra-right adherents of Anthroposophy today are officials of the World League for the Protection of Life (WSL), a small but influential and very wealthy environmental organization in the Federal Republic. The garden at its educational center is cultivated according to biodynamic methods, and visitors are served organic refreshments. Yet this organization was founded in 1958 by former members of the National Socialist party, and today it links protection of 'life' (that is, 'right-to-life') themes and the environment with racism and a revival of *völkisch* ideology. The 'life' it is most interested in protecting is of course German 'life'; thus the WSL is rabidly anti-abortion, believing that German women should be devoted to giving birth to 'Aryan' babies.

The spiritual leader of the WSL and its key figure for most of its history has been Werner Georg Haverbeck. Born in 1909, Haverbeck became an active Nazi at an early age; it should be recalled that Nazism was largely a youth movement, so that members like Haverbeck are still alive. [33] Haverbeck joined the SA in 1928 and from 1929 to 1932 was a member of the Reich Administration for the National Socialist Student League (Reichsleitung der NSDAP-Studentenschaft) and a leader of the Reich Youth Leadership of the Hitler Youth (Reichjugendführung der Hitlerjugend). He served as a leading official of the Strength Through Joy organization, which controlled recreational activities under the Third Reich; in 1933 Rudolf Hess saw to it that Haverbeck's passport was stamped "This man is not to be arrested." He survived the Röhm purge to help organize the Nuremberg Party Congress and join Hess's staff. It was Hess who converted him to Anthroposophy. During the war he conducted radio propaganda in Denmark and worked in South America; by the end of the war he was an officer.[34]

After the Allies rudely aborted Haverbeck's many efforts on behalf of the Third Reich, he contented himself for a time working as a pastor for the Anthroposophical Christian community. He founded an educational center called the Collegium Humanum in 1963, where today ecofascist, esoteric, *völkisch*, Anthroposophist, neopagan, and primitivist groups meet and hold workshops. He co-founded the WSL and served as its president from 1974 to 1982. In 1981, he was a signatory of the notorious Heidelberg Manifesto, a document drawn up by a group of professors to warn the German people of the dangers that immigration posed to them. Its first draft began:

> With great concern we observe the subversion of the German people through the influx of many millions of foreigners and their families, the foreignization of our language, our culture, and our nationhood. . . . Already many Germans have become foreigners in their living districts and workplaces, and thus in their own *Heimat*.[35]

Routine as this language may sound now, when opposition to immigration in the Federal Republic is much more tolerated and neofascists pander to it relentlessly, the Manifesto had to be toned down at the time (1981) because of the public outcry it raised.

In accordance with Anthroposophical root-race beliefs, Haverbeck is notable for propounding the thesis that the two world wars in this century in fact constituted a thirty years' war waged by foreign aggressors against the German people and their spiritual life. Apparently, German spiritual life stood in the way of "the strivings for world domination by the Anglo-Saxon race," behind which lay "the intensive image of a call to world dominance, like the old Jewish consciousness." Indeed, Haverbeck maintains, the two world wars amounted to a conspiracy against the German people and spiritual life. It is a "historical lie" that the Nazis ran "mass-murder camps," argues Haverbeck, and is actually "enemy propaganda." It was Russia that was the aggressor in the Second World War.[36]

In his 1989 book *Rudolf Steiner: Advocate for Germany,*
Haverbeck lauds Steiner (who died in 1925) for understanding
the existence of this ongoing conspiracy early on.

> During the first world war, Rudolf Steiner delivered a
> multitude of lectures about contemporary history, and
> he toiled inexhaustibly for the truth about the question
> of "war guilt." . . . Steiner presented his listeners with
> maps that showed that goals that had been proclaimed
> back in 1889 were being fulfilled [during World War I].
> These maps anticipated the separation of Central Eu-
> rope that would be ultimately achieved with the loss of
> East Germany. . . . What was not fully achieved through
> the Versailles treaty in 1919 was in fact completed in
> 1945: the demolition of Germany. . . . The leading forces
> of both parties to the cold war were united in this
> common struggle against spiritual Germany. "This war
> [World War I] was a conspiracy against German spiri-
> tual life," said Steiner. [37]

When Haverbeck's book on Steiner's nationalism was published, it caused an outcry of protest among outraged
countercultural Anthroposophists who send their children to
Waldorf Schools, use Demeter products, and are in no way
racists or fascists. Yet as researcher Wölk points out, their
protests were unwarranted, since Haverbeck was only presenting Steiner as what he actually was — "a crude nationalist whose
demonizations were shared by the *völkisch* groups of his day" —
to show his usefulness for nationalist and neofascist groups
today.[38]

This alleged conspiracy against German spiritual life per-
vades much of the WSL's current thinking, notes Wölk. WSLers
consider the "flood of asylum-seekers," the destruction of the
environment, and the ongoing transformation of the Federal
Republic into a multicultural society to be part of the spiritual
war against the Germans. They regard the protection of the
environment as part of the protection of a people, of its biological "substance" and its national identity. Indeed, WSLers see the
battle for a healthy environment as part of the all-encompassing

spiritual struggle against the homogenizing forces of modernity and "Western civilization." Haverbeck's wife, Ursula Haverbeck-Wetzel, another former WSL president who "for religious reasons refuses to dissociate herself from any human being, including Adolf Hitler,"[39] observes:

> Whenever a person comes to feel that he belongs to the cultural strain that is deeply rooted in his people which has not only a material existence but a spiritual reality that is superior to the material plane — he has broken out from being a manipulated consumer. He has escaped the mass homogenization of completely manipulated people who are "amusing themselves to death" (as Neil Postman put it), which is the goal of "One World" advocates, intent on power and domination. The person who is faithful to his religious convictions and attentive and caring to his culture and customs, they consider dangerous.[40]

Ernst Otto Cohrs, the WSL's president since 1989, is another devotee of Rudolf Steiner, having been an Anthroposophist since 1961. Today Cohrs's interests seem to lie in promulgating race theories, and publishing and distributing anti-Semitic literature. In 1982, an official of the WSL's Bavarian chapter made a public issue of Cohrs's activities inside the WSL. He wrote a letter to a WSL membership assembly saying that it should dissociate itself from Cohrs because, among other things, he was sending anti-Semitic literature to WSL members, running advertisements in ultra-right magazines like *Bauernschaft* (the journal of the notorious Holocaust-denier Thies Christophersen), permitting neofascist periodicals to reprint WSL leaflets, and himself distributing such writings as *There Were No Gas Chambers* and *The Auschwitz Myth*.[41] Many members withdrew from the WSL as a result of this letter; those who remained were overwhelmingly those who shared Cohrs's anti-Semitic ideas and were not disposed to contradict him. Among them was Baldur Springmann, the 'ecofarmer' who was involved in the Greens in the early days, whose book *Partner Erde* (Partner Earth) was published by an ultra-right publisher (Arndt Verlag), and who writes for the 'New' Right publication *Nation Europa;* and Dr. Arnold Neugebohrn, a Republican candidate for the provincial legislature who takes pride in his NSDAP 'gold medal.' Concludes Wölk, "The internal crisis caused by Cohrs's activities in 1981-82 may have diminished the ranks of the WSL, but it also strengthened the WSL's neofascist orientation." Cohrs's current activities are still primarily the dissemination of Holocaust-denial literature.[42]

One collective member of the WSL is a Hamburg-based organization known as the Society for Biological Anthropology, Eugenics, and Behavioral Research (Gesellschaft für biologische Anthropologie, Eugenik, und Verhaltensforschung, or GfbAEV), whose head is Jürgen Rieger, a "neo-Nazi in lawyer's robes" (as the newspaper *Die Zeit* called him) who is currently defending two fascist groups that the Federal Republic banned in 1992; one of the GfbAEV's fellows is the leading ideologue of the French Nouvelle Droite, Alain de Benoist. Its periodical is the notorious quarterly journal *Neue Anthropologie,* which maintains, among other things, that there has always been environmental destruction in the history of humanity, that in fact one could even say this was part of human nature were it not for one sole exception:

> Only the Germans were different. In pagan times they worshipped groves and trees, and because of their closeness to nature, they had a caring orientation toward nature. Even the love of animals is much more pronounced among the Germanic peoples than it is, for example, among the Romance-language-speaking peoples. It is thus no coincidence that even today the most stalwart environmentalist efforts — private as well as state — are those conducted by peoples who have a larger proportion of the Nordic race.[43]

RUDOLF BAHRO: *VÖLKISCH* SPIRITUALITY

If fascists are using ecological themes to update their racial and nationalist aims, other thinkers are developing an ecological spiritualism along New Age lines that bears no small resemblance to the *völkisch* Germanic spirituality of the 1920s. Indeed, "a great part of the literature about close-to-nature spirituality that the alternative scene is reading is permeated with reactionary, *völkisch*, or even National Socialist content," writes Ditfurth. "We find neofascist and ultra-right positions not only in the various political and even ecological groups, but also . . . in neopagan, esoteric and occult circles."[44]

Perhaps the most prominent figure in this connection is Rudolf Bahro. Many German 'new social movement' circles previously accepted Bahro as a social theorist contributing to a 'socialism with a human face' and continue to regard him as part of the independent left; leftist periodicals publish uncritical interviews with him. In the Anglo-American world, too, many ecological radicals still consider Bahro as representing something 'leftist.' Yet Bahro no longer considers himself a leftist; indeed, he is a vehement critic of the left[45] and of "comrades without fatherland."[46] In fact, as antifascist researcher Roger Niedenführ argues, since the mid-1980s Bahro has been contributing to the development of a "spiritual fascism" that has the effect of "rehabilitating National Socialism," openly calling for reclaiming the "positive" side of the Nazi movement. Not only does Bahro appeal to a mystical Germanist spirituality like the *völkisch* ideologues of the 1920s, he even sees the need for a "Green Adolf" who will lead Germans out of their own "folk-depths" and into ecological "salvation."

Bahro originally became well known as the author of *The Alternative in Eastern Europe*, which he wrote during the 1970s while he was a dissident Marxist and party member in the former East Germany. In 1977, the ruling Communist government sentenced him to prison; in 1979, he was deported. Once arrived in what was then West Germany, Bahro became involved with the nascent German Greens, affirming that "red and green go well together."[48] In the early 1980s peace movement, he alarmed many by enunciating nationalistic arguments against the deployment of Pershing missiles. [49] He began to speak less in political terms and more in religious terms, asking that "the emphasis [be] shifted from politics and the question of power towards the cultural level...to the prophetic level....Our aim has to be the 'reconstruction of God.'"[50] He became a vocal 'fundamentalist' critic of the *realo* wing of the Greens (those who became generally committed to exercising parliamentary power) and ultimately left the party in 1985. In a parting speech in Hamburg, he said there were structural similarities between the Greens and the Nazi movement that the Greens were not taking advantage of but should; then he gave his 'fundamentalist' alternative: "the other republic that we want will be an association of communities of life-communities in which God and Goddess are at the center."[51]

Bahro thereafter moved increasingly toward the New Age esoteric milieu. His major concern remained "the ecological crisis," whose "deep structures" must be investigated, but he now thinks ecology "has nothing to do with left and right."[52] Today Bahro is one of the leading spokespeople and theorists of New Age ideas in the Federal Republic. "The most important thing," he rambles,

> is that . . . [people] take the path "back" and align themselves with the Great Equilibrium, in the harmony between the human order and the Tao of life. I think the "esoteric"-political theme of "king and queen of the world" is basically the question of how men and women are to comprehend and interact with each other in a spiritually comprehensive way. Whoever does not bring themselves to cooperate with the world government [*Weltregierung*] will get their due.[53]

In 1989, Bahro cofounded a combination educational center and commune near Trier, the Lernwerkstatt (an "ecological academy for one world"), whose purpose is to synthesize spirituality and politics, "to come to a new personal and social orientation." It presents lectures, cultural events, and weekend workshops on various New Age themes, including deep ecology, ecofeminism, Zen Buddhism, holistic nutrition, Sufism, and the like — as well as German identity.[54] His 1987 book *Logik der Rettung* marked an overt embrace of authoritarian theological concepts that shocked many former admirers.[55]

Bahro also holds a professorship at Humboldt University in Berlin, where he conducts a seminar whose sessions are usually filled to overflowing. At Humboldt, he holds a chair in 'social ecology,' and he refers to his 'science' by this name, but Bahro's work is not to be confused with the social ecology conceived and developed by Murray Bookchin. Although the two theorists agree that class contradictions are not the exclusive social contradiction, Bookchin regards hierarchy as basic, while emphasizing the importance of class interests. Bahro, by contrast, points to "tribal consciousness" as rooted "more deeply than class consciousness," even in the spiritually "deepest layers" of a people. "The national question is an objective reality," Bahro says, that is on a much "deeper basis than the class question."[56]

Moreover, whereas Bookchin's consistently internationalist social ecology affirms reason and naturalism and repeatedly criticizes ecomysticism and ecotheology, Bahro's version of 'social ecology' is overwhelmingly spiritualistic. Indeed, in late 1990, when Bookchin spoke at the Humboldt seminar at Bahro's invitation, Bahro told Bookchin that his (Bahro's) own 'social ecology' was actually an attempt to synthesize Bookchin's social ecology with deep ecology.[57] Politics must be based on spiritualistic values today, in Bahro's view, because "without a return to the spiritual source," politics "will not be worthy of that name."[58] Not only are those who see spirituality and politics as opposites fundamentally wrong, he argues, but our global ecological problems are in fact a material reflection of the inner spiritual "sickness" that separates them. It is a religious "politics of consciousness" — that is, the implanting of spiritualistic ideas — that can arrest the global ecological crisis and prepare people for the new political order.[59]

Bahro's spiritualistic approach has a distinctly ethno-cultural dimension. He speaks of peoples as if they had unique spiritual 'essences' that are indissoluble, that cannot be destroyed over time.[60] He is particularly concerned with the 'German essence' (*deutsche Wesenheit*) and its various manifestations on the material plane.[61] In approaching the ecological crisis, the German 'essence' demands the incorporation of spiritualism, particularly the mystical tradition initiated by Meister Eckhart, whom "we Germans should read."[62] Bahro favorably contrasts this "German legacy"[63] with socialism and the Enlightenment.

It appears not to alarm Bahro, as antifascist researcher Peter Kratz points out, that his mystical Germanism closely resembles the mystical Germanism of the *völkisch* movement.[64] Bahro, in fact, consciously associates himself with the *völkisch* movement —he says he wants an "awakening in the *Volk*"[65]—and with the 1920s Conservative Revolution against the Enlightenment generally.[66] Indeed, Bahro is critical of the Greens, among other things, because they did "not attend to this *völkisch* moment."[67] Kratz warns that this gives Bahro's approach "the same potential for political catastrophe that the *völkisch* movement had, even though this would please Bahro as little as it would have pleased the originators of the *völkisch* movement."[68]

'Essences' like the 'German essence' cannot remain in the spiritual plane; they must be manifested in concrete reality — that is, in politics, history, and society. In Bahro's prospectus (and in stark contrast to Bookchin's anarchist libertarian municipalism), these manifestations will not take the form of democratic institutions, since "to say that we will create grassroots democracy now, among these wolves, is nonsense."[69] Bahro criticizes the "bean-counting voting" process of democracy and prefers a spiritual consensus process for decision making.[70] Although he is currently receiving state support from Saxony for an eco-communal demonstration project (thanks largely to his friend and visiting lecturer at Humboldt, Saxon prime minister Kurt Biedenkopf), Bahro also rejects the state: "Society's rule of law," he asserts, "may no longer be based on the state or on any other existing forces that are even less legitimate."[71]

Despite his antistatist assertions, which may make him appear attractively anti-authoritarian, like many 'New' Rightists Bahro expressly believes that the ecological crisis is resolvable only through authoritarian means. He calls for a spiritually based and hierarchically elitist "salvation government" (*Rettungsregierung*) or a "god-state" (*Gottesstaat*)[72] that will be run by a "new political authority at the highest level": a "prince of the ecological turn."[73] The "prince," which apparently may be a collective entity, will constitute a spiritual elite, an oligarchy responsible only to God. As a "voice of the divine,"[74] this guru elite will dictate the law of God and nature, in order to convert the present society to the "order according to nature"[75] that Bahro sees as desirable. People should not "be afraid" of the advent of this "prince," says Bahro, since "a bit of 'ecodictatorship' is needed" to handle our problems today.[76] Besides, "it is a matter of absolute indifference whether [this prince] is a man or a woman," he assures us, "it is a question of structure. That is the German moment in this Green movement."[77] But today it is important to develop a broad spiritual consciousness in the general population, for "without a spiritual determination, there will be no new redemptive institutionalization" — that is, no "prince."[78] It is presumably cheering that "in spite of all bad experiences... the strongest political-psychological dispositions of our people" make "the Germans more responsive than other peoples to charismatic leadership."[79]

Liberating the 'Brown Parts'

Since the mid-1980s, Bahro has been remarkably open about proclaiming his embrace of the spiritual content of fascism for the 'salvation' of nature and humanity. In *The Logic of Salvation*, he asks, "Is there really no thought more reprehensible than a new 1933?" — that is, Hitler's rise to state power. "But that is precisely what can save us! The ecology and peace movement is the first popular German movement since the Nazi movement. It must co-redeem [*miterlösen*] Hitler."[80] Indeed, "the Nazi movement [was] among other things an early reading of the ecology movement."[81] Germans are to look for "the positive that may lie buried in the Nazi movement" and reclaim it, he says, "because if we do not, we will remain cut off from our roots, the roots from which will grow that which will save us."[82] Today one must "liberate" the "brown parts" in the German character.[83] The fact is, says Bahro, that today "there is a call in the depths of the *Volk* for a Green Adolf."[84]

When Bahro's critics reproach him for this assertion, Bahro responds that no, he does not mean Adolf *Hitler*. That his leftist critics think he means Adolf *Hitler* shows that the left "responds only with fear, instead of comprehending that a Green Adolf would be an entirely different Adolf from the one we know about."[85] Yet as Kratz points out, Bahro himself is evasive about what this 'Green Adolf' actually would be: perhaps a personified *Führer*, perhaps a spiritual elite, or perhaps some inner self-recognition that within each of us there is supposedly a 'Green Adolf,' to whom we must subordinate ourselves voluntarily through spiritual insight. This evasiveness is itself a matter of concern. Kratz believes that Bahro really means a personified *Führer*; for one thing, Bahro invokes the 'sleeping emperor' myth,[86] the nationalistic notion that the Emperor Barbarossa is sleeping in the Kyffhäuser Mountain and will one day come back as the *Führer* and rescue Germany from dire straits[87] — an idea that is also one of the foundations of the Nazi *Führer* principle.

For Bahro, this *Führer* will clearly be a spiritualistic leader. In a foreword to a book by his colleague Jochen Kirchhoff, he argued that National Socialism had had the right spiritual aims: it sought to manifest the 'German essence' on the material plane. It went wrong in the execution — for one thing, it was very violent. But even this was understandable since, arising as it did in the 1920s, it was the task of National Socialism to make the first real spiritual revolt against the overwhelming materialism of the age. Thus, the materialistic thinking of the Weimar era, against which National Socialism rebelled, was the real cause of the Nazis' material "vehemence"— that is, mass murder.[88]

The materialistic thinking of Weimar modernity that the Nazis were so correct to oppose, says Bahro, is also today the immediate cause of the ecological crisis. Only the spiritualization of consciousness, Bahro believes, can prevail over biosphere-destroying materialism. Hence Germans today have no alternative but to invoke the spiritually "deep forces" from the Nazi movement — in order to "be present with our whole potential."[89]

But it must be a strictly spiritual endeavor: undertaking concrete political resistance on the material plane is, for Bahro, itself an integral component of materialistic secularism, an expression of negative spirituality. Those who engage in politics on the material plane today, he says, in fact politically resemble — Nazis! True, the Nazis had to struggle in the twenties, but at least they had the right spiritual ideas. But "revolt (under the conditions of our imperial situation) is fascistic. That is to say, it redeems [*rettet*] nothing."[90] Bahro's religious dispensation thus does not synthesize spirituality and politics at all, as critic

Niedenführ points out; on the contrary, it simply eliminates political action.[91]

Repelled by these ideas, critics have denounced *The Logic of Salvation* as fascistic or 'fascistoid' — potentially fascist. Bahro responds that such "faint-hearted antifascism" has "refused" to "look for the strength that lay beneath the brown movement."[92] Precisely because the left rejects the insights of spirituality, it can never see the necessity of *völkisch*-authoritarian structures and therefore can never give material form to the 'German essence,' he believes. Bahro replied further in his next book, *Rückkehr*:

> It can be instructive that there was a strong wing of the Nazis that wanted to be socially and culturally revolutionary. This wing was not consolidated, and the Hitler movement went on to serve a regenerated German capitalism. . . . We can no longer allow fascism to be a taboo subject.

It should be noted that fascism has hardly been a 'taboo subject' in the Federal Republic — on the contrary, it has been much discussed. What has been rightly rejected — and hardly merely 'taboo,' since a taboo begs to be broken — is sympathy for the Nazis. Bahro continues:

> I can't rule out the possibility that at the end of the 1920s I wouldn't have gone with the Nazis. And it's very important that we be prepared to ask such a question. As for what would have happened later, I don't know. There were people in the Nazi movement who gave it up before 1933; there were people who saw the light with the Röhm affair; some went into the resistance; others were executed. But we're not supposed to imagine what we ourselves would have done. And I was ready and am ready to go into such questions. I think that if we are serious about forming a popular movement and overcoming the ecological crisis, and if we are really to address what comes out of the depths, we will have to have a lot to do with what it was that found expression then and that is seeking another, better expression this

time. That can go well only if there is a great deal of consciousness about whatever unhappy mechanisms lie in all of us, the resentment reactions, mere rebellion instead of revolution.[93]

Posing as a courageous inquiry into the breaking of taboos, such practices do nothing more than give people permission to envision themselves as Nazis — a horrifying dispensation in any era, but particularly in one when present-day Nazis routinely attack foreigners in German towns and cities and when fascist parties are having electoral victories.

Some of Bahro's associates add to the strong suspicion that his 'Green Adolf' refers to a new *Führer*. One of his fellow teachers at the Lernwerkstatt, for example, is Rainer Langhans, a former anarchistic 'wild man' of the 1960s German student organization SDS who writes today that "spirituality in Germany is named Hitler. And only when you have gone a little bit further can you go beyond it. Until then, however, you must reclaim the inheritance . . . not in the sense of this fine exclusionary antifascism but in the sense of further developing what Hitler tried to do." And: "This dumb Enlightenment, which builds up dams against so-called 'outbreaks of the irrational,' is actually merely laughable as an antifascist syndrome." And: "We have to be, so to speak, the better fascists."[94] Another of Bahro's fellow teachers at the Lernwerkstatt is Jochen Kirchhoff, who writes that "National Socialism was a botched attempt at healing the world . . . and to ground politics in the spiritual."[95]

To speak at his seminar at Humboldt, Bahro also invited Wolfgang Deppert, a onetime head of the *völkisch*-racist sect German Unitary Religion Community (DUR), even though at the end of 1990 Deppert permitted the publication in one of his periodicals of an article by Princess Marie-Adelheld Reuss-zur-Lippe. Earlier in her life, in the 1920s, this person was a founder of the 'Nordic Ring' and later a close political and personal confidante of the Third Reich's Agriculture Minister, Walther Darré, who called her "my little sister." In 1985, she was the editor-in-chief of the journal *Bauernschaft (Peasantry)*, whose publisher is Thies Christophersen, the notorious author of the despicable 1973 pamphlet *Die Auschwitz Lüge (The Auschwitz*

Lie).[96] Deppert, apparently, spoke at the Humboldt seminar on philosophy and science.

But whatever happened at that lecture, Murray Bookchin's appearance at the seminar on November 21, 1990, did not go over well with the host. Bahro had asked Bookchin to address such questions as "Is the alternative to ecological destruction freedom from domination or an 'ecological' dictatorship?" Bookchin replied that "an 'ecological' dictatorship would not be ecological — it would finally finish off the planet altogether. It would be the glorification, the hypostasization, of social control, of manipulation, the objectification of human beings, the denial of human freedom and selfconsciousness, in the name of ecological problems. . . . An 'ecological' dictatorship is a contradiction in terms, an oxymoron."

When Bookchin had finished his presentation, the following exchange took place:

> **Bahro:** You put such a spotlight on the positive side of human nature — cooperation and so on — that if that were true, it's improbable that again and again we would have fallen back into egotism and competition. You see human nature predominantly as positive. But more often than not, it has worked out for the worse rather than for the better. Most often the institutions that the human species has created have had hierarchy and domination. The fact that they did so must have a foundation in human nature. . . .
>
> When you talk about rationality, *Geist,* the fully developed capacity of being human, you are confronting this side least — the "dark side." Because that is what gives us the capacity to dominate, this *Geist,* our rationality. You don't want to confront that as fundamental. . . .
>
> **Bookchin:** I don't ignore the "dark side" of humanity. . . . But if the "dark side" exists everywhere, then why has it been necessary for the "dark side" to express itself in institutions of the most barbarous kind? Why did there have to be coercion? Why does that "dark side" always have to be institutionalized through force, through

superstition, through fear, through threat, and through ideologies of the most barbarous nature? . . . There's no question that there is a "dark side" to human history. . . . But it's very hard to find the biological reasons for that "dark side." Because that "dark side" has always operated through the institutions of a minority who relied on force and depended on propaganda and superstition, and on the worst things that the human mind can develop, to suppress the millions and millions.

Bahro: But does it have natural foundations?

Bookchin: It emerges from a social foundation. . . . If the "dark side" is natural, why is it that in all the great revolutions that we know of, people have broken out with a generosity of spirit that is incredible? They have been willing to trust, to care, to feel the pain even of their masters — when their masters tried to oppress them, owing to their own insecurities. . . . In warrior societies, to make the adolescent transformation into a warrior, you have to inflict pain upon him. You have to spoil him, to make him a sufferer in order to make him part of the community of warriors. . . . I don't see the "dark side" of human nature, but of social nature.[97]

After Bookchin gave his lecture, Bahro told Bookchin that he would not invite him to speak again.

SOCIAL DARWINIST 'ECOLOGY': HERBERT GRUHL

Bahro, let it be said, claims to look for the roots of the ecological crisis in the "sickness" in "white Nordic humanity." But the far right most often locates these roots in non-Europeans and uses 'ecology' to marshal classic racist arguments against Third World immigration. In the "Europe of fatherlands" of the "ethnopluralism" concept, each *Volk* requires its own specific, familiar home environment in order to thrive. Interference from outside — including immigration — disturbs that natural environment, the "natural ecology of the *Volk.*" Most often, the far right claims to be defending cultures rather than races; if the Nazis persecuted those who practiced 'race mixing' and sought to preserve 'racial purity,' today's fascists say they oppose *cultural* mixing and seek to preserve their *culture*. Thus, the ecofascist and misleadingly named Ecological Democratic Party (Ökologische Demokratische Partei, or ÖDP) calls for "asylum-seekers [to] be accepted by countries that belong to the same *cultural* area as the asylum seekers themselves," and they call for "*Heimat* instead of multiculture."[98]

The hollowness of such claims becomes evident, however, when they are clothed in terms of 'ecology.' For the far right's notion of ecology is in fact nothing more than social Darwinism, the reactionary ideology that biology dictates the form of society, that genes rather than environment determine culture. Social Darwinist 'ecology' can then advance seemingly 'ecological' reasons for keeping out immigrants and for asserting ethnic or national identity — while avoiding the terminology of race.

Social Darwinism has deep roots in the German ultra-right. When it first emerged as a doctrine in the nineteenth century, its German form was very different from its Anglo-American form. Like Anglo-American social Darwinism, German social Darwinism projected human social institutions onto the nonhuman world as 'natural laws,' then invoked those 'laws' to justify the human social arrangements as 'natural.' It also applied the maxim 'survival of the fittest' to society. But where Anglo-American social Darwinism conceived the 'fittest' as the individual entrepreneur in a 'bloody tooth and claw' capitalist jungle, German social Darwinism overwhelmingly conceived the 'fittest' in terms of race. Thus, the 'fittest' race not only would but should survive, vanquishing all its competitors in its 'struggle for existence.' As historian Daniel Gasman observes:

> It may be said that if Darwinism in England was an extension of *laissez faire* individualism projected from the social world to the natural world, [in Germany it was] a projection of German romanticism and philosophical idealism.... The form which social Darwinism took in Germany was a pseudo-scientific religion of

nature worship and nature-mysticism combined with notions of racism.[99]

Since this social Darwinism seemed to give a 'scientific' basis to racism, National Socialism drew heavily on it to provide 'scientific' grounds for its virulent racism. Hitler wrote in *Mein Kampf*, for example, that people "owe their higher existence, not to the ideas of a few crazy ideologists, but to the knowledge and ruthless application of Nature's stern and rigid laws." Among these 'laws': "Nature usually makes certain corrective decisions with regard to the racial purity of earthly creatures. She has little love for bastards."[100] To establish their totalitarian regime and implement genocide, the Nazis easily drew on the common ideology that the *Volk* mediates between individual and cosmos, rendering the individual mainly a member of a larger whole, the '*Volk* whole' or '*Volk* community.'

It is well known among ecological activists today that Ernst Haeckel coined the term *ecology* in the 1860s; what is less known is that Haeckel was the primary spokesperson for German social Darwinism in the latter half of the nineteenth century, as Gasman shows. German social Darwinism was thus almost immediately married to the concept of ecology. Haeckel was also a believer in mystical racism and nationalism, so that German social Darwinism was from the beginning a political concept that lent romantic racism and nationalism a pseudo-biological basis. In fact, as Gasman argues,

> racially inspired social Darwinism in Germany . . . was almost completely indebted to Haeckel for its creation. . . . His ideas served to unite into a full-bodied ideology the trends of racism, imperialism, romanticism, anti-Semitism and nationalism. . . . It was Haeckel who brought the full weight of science down hard on the side of what were Volkism's essentially irrational and mystical ideas.[101]

Haeckel himself was a proponent of carrying over concepts like 'selective breeding' and 'racial hygiene' from nonhuman nature into human society.

Despite the widely different scientific concepts of ecology that have emerged since Haeckel's day, the 'ecology' that today's ecofascists draw upon is essentially the social Darwinism of Haeckel. Perhaps the most prominent social Darwinist-'ecological' racist in Germany today is Herbert Gruhl,[102] a former Christian Democrat parliamentarian whose best-selling 1975 book, *A Planet Is Plundered: The Balance of Terror of Our Politics*, makes an explicit social Darwinist interpretation of ecology.[103] In the late 1970s and early 1980s Gruhl participated in the formation of the German Greens with a new political group he had founded, Green Action Future (GAZ). It was Gruhl who created the slogan "We are neither left nor right; we are in front," according to Charlene Spretnak and Fritjof Capra.[104] In the early 1980s, ultrarightists, including Gruhl's GAZ, struggled with leftists and centrists for the direction of the Green Party; the center-left ultimately took control. "It is to the credit of the leftist tendencies in the founding phases of the Greens," writes Ditfurth, "that the ultra-right and neofascists were prevented from taking over ecological politics, as they were threatening to do at the time."[105]

Gruhl, on the losing end, concluded that the Greens had given up their "concern for ecology in favor of a leftist ideology of emancipation" and walked out of the party. He continued his fight for his conception of ecology outside the Greens, however; with his fellow ultra-rightist Baldur Springmann, he founded the Ecological Democratic Party (ÖDP) in 1982 and wrote most of its programmatic literature, orienting ecology toward fascism and endowing racism and population policy with an 'ecological' legitimation. In 1989, when an ÖDP party congress dared to pass a resolution formally distancing the party from the NPD and the Republicans, this 'leftist victory' was too much for Gruhl, and he left to form yet another group. Since the mid-1980s, Gruhl has appeared as a guest speaker at various neo-Nazi and Holocaust-denial events and continues to publish books on 'ecology.'

Gruhl's social Darwinist 'ecology' reduces human beings to their biological attributes and applies the 'laws' of nature to society: "All laws that apply to living nature generally apply to people as well, since people themselves are part of living nature," he maintains.[107] These 'natural laws' dictate that people should accept the present social order as it is. Domination, hierarchy, and exploitation should be accepted, since "the swan is white, without anyone artificially cleaning it. The raven is black, and everything is in its natural place of its own accord. This is good. All the strivings of people . . . for organized justice are simply hopeless."[108] People should adapt to existing conditions instead of making futile attempts to change them, since "every life-form accommodates itself to that which it cannot change."[109]

If society were set up according to nature, Gruhl believes, cultures would institute prescriptions against those who deviate from their existing norms, since "in the hunting grounds of the wilderness, if an animal breaks the unwritten law of the herd and goes its own way, it generally pays for this independence with its life."[110] Moreover, cultures should be kept separate from one another: "When many cultures are all jumbled together in the same area, the result will be that they live alongside each other, in conflict with each other, or . . . they will undergo entropy, becoming a mixture whose value lessens with every intermixing, until in the last analysis it has no more worth." The reason for cultural separation too has its basis in 'natural law,' "a law of entropy which we particularly have in ecology, and this law also holds for human cultures."[111]

In the coming years, Gruhl believes that cultures around the globe will compete for survival over the means of life, in a social Darwinist struggle for existence. "There is no doubt that the wars of the future will be fought over shares in the basic foundations of life — that is, over the basis of nutrition and the increasingly precious fruits of the soil. Under these circumstances, future wars will far surpass in frightfulness all previous wars."[112] The peoples who have the best prospects for survival will be those who are best armed and who best conserve their resources; those who "succeed in bringing their military preparedness to the highest level, while keeping their standard of living low, will have an enormous advantage."[113]

In the interests of this struggle, Germans must not only arm themselves but preserve their environment by keeping the number of people who inhabit it down: "Violations of ecological equilibrium and the destruction of natural living spaces [*Lebensräume*] are directly related to population density."

"Overpopulation" in the Third World, however, has produced "armies of job-seekers" who are entering Germany with a "capacity for annihilation" comparable to a "nuclear bomb," Gruhl writes. This "tidal wave of humanity" is a primary menace that will cause "all order to break down" in Europe. Third World immigrants are thus threatening European culture itself, which will "perish not because of the degeneration of its own people, as previous high civilizations have, but because of physical laws: the constantly overflowing mass of humanity on an earth's surface that remains constant."[115] Therefore, there is no room for immigrants in the Federal Republic: "Because of its high population density, the Federal Republic of Germany, one of the most densely settled countries on earth, cannot be a destination country for immigrants. We therefore reject the unlimited acceptance of foreigners."[116] Accordingly, Gruhl demands "an end to immigration for ecological reasons." [117]

The 'laws of nature,' for Gruhl, offer a solution to Third World immigration, especially the 'law' that "the only acceptable currency with which violations of natural law can be paid for is death. Death brings the equalization; it cuts back all life that has overgrown on this planet, so that the planet can once again come into equilibrium."[118] Fortunately, in his view, Third World people will accept this lethal solution since their lives "rest on a completely different basic outlook on life from our own: their own death, like that of their children, is accepted as fate."[119]

Needless to say, Gruhl does not think democracy is the most efficient way to address these problems. After all, this situation "will take on the proportions of an emergency in coming years, and attempts that will be made to prevail in it will produce a permanent state of emergency."[120] In an interview with the editors of *Junge Freiheit (Young Freedom)*, the flagship publication of the National Revolutionaries, Gruhl was asked whether the problems of protecting the environment and life can be solved within a democracy. "Probably not," he replied, "because democracies follow the Zeitgeist, and in all countries of the world today the Zeitgeist is to raise the standard of living further. Parties that warn about this and advocate renunciation of consumption seem to have little chance." Instead, Gruhl demands a "strong state," strong both internationally and domestically — if possible, even a state with "dictatorial powers."[121]

In the autumn of 1991, the environmental minister of Lower Saxony shocked many observers by awarding Herbert Gruhl a highly prestigious state honor. "With his international best-seller *A Planet Is Plundered*," minister Monika Greifahn said, Gruhl has "placed ideas of environmental protection and care at the forefront of public political consciousness."[122]

A Social Ecology of Freedom

A combination of nationalism, authoritarianism, and yearnings for charismatic leaders that is legitimated by a mystical and biologistic 'ecology' is potentially socially catastrophic. Just as the *völkisch* movement ultimately was channeled into the Nazi movement, so too new social movements that appeal to these concepts must be mindful of their potential for political and social catastrophe if they are channeled into a dangerous political direction that draws on mysticism.

A love of the natural world and alienation from modern society are in themselves innocent and legitimate ideas, and it was by no means a historical necessity that they be permutated into a justification for mass murder. Nor is 'ecology' limited to an interpretation as a social Darwinist racial jungle, or politicized along tribal, regional, and nationalist lines. Nor is 'ecology' inherently an antirational, mystical concept. Finally, the ecological crisis can hardly be dismissed; it is itself very real and is worsening rapidly. Indeed, the politicization of ecology is not only desirable but necessary.

Although this article has focused on the 'ecological' right in the Federal Republic, 'ecological' fascism is hardly limited to that country. In Britain, a wing of the National Front issues the cry, "Racial preservation is Green!" In the United States, the notorious white supremacist Tom Metzger remarks:

> I've noticed that there's an increased number of young people in the white racialist movement who are also quite interested in ecology, protecting the animals from cruelty and things like that, and it seems to me that as we

are becoming more aware of our precarious state, the white man, the white woman's, state in the world, being only about 10 percent of the population, we begin to sympathize, empathize more, with the wolves and other animals.[123]

His colleague Monique Wolfing agrees: "Well, naturally. They're in the same position we are. Why would we want something created for ourselves and yet watch nature be destroyed? We work hand in hand with nature and we should save nature along with trying to save our race."[124] The noted U.S. deep ecologist Bill Devall, who is certainly not a fascist, has allowed anti-immigration themes to enter his views: He notes with apparent relief that while "population is beginning to stabilize in Western Europe and North America," there is a caveat — "in-migration." Devall chastises those who would "justify large-scale in-migration to Western Europe and North America from Latin America and Africa" as guilty of "misplaced humanism."[125]

What is clearly crucial is how an ecological politics is conceived. If the Green slogan "we are neither left nor right but up front" was ever meaningful, the emergence of an 'ecological right' defines the slogan's bankruptcy conclusively. The need for an ecological left is urgent, especially one that is firmly committed to a clear, coherent set of anticapitalist, democratic, antihierarchical views. It must have firm roots in the internationalism of the left and the rational, humanistic, and genuinely egalitarian critique of social oppression that was part of the Enlightenment, particularly its revolutionary libertarian offshoot.

But an ecologically oriented politics must deal with biological phenomena warily, since interpretations of them can serve sinister ends. When 'respect for Nature' comes to mean 'reverence,' it can mutate ecological politics into a religion that 'Green Adolfs' can effectively use for authoritarian ends. When 'Nature,' in turn, becomes a metaphor legitimating sociobiology's 'morality of the gene,' the glories of 'racial purity,' 'love of *Heimat*,' 'woman equals nature,' or 'Pleistocene consciousness,' the cultural setting is created for reaction. 'Ecological' fascism is a cynical but potentially politically effective attempt to mystically link genuine concern for present-day environmental problems with time-honored fears of the 'outsider' or the 'new,' indeed the best elements of the Enlightenment, through ecological verbiage. Authoritarian mystifications need not be the fate of today's ecology movement, as social ecology demonstrates. But they could become its fate if ecomystics, ecoprimitivists, misanthropes, and antirationalists have their way.

FOOTNOTES

1. On social ecology, see the many writings of Murray Bookchin, particularly *Remaking Society* (Boston: South End Press, 1989) and *Urbanization Without Cities* (Montreal: Black Rose Books, 1992).

2. Jutta Ditfurth, *Feuer in die Herzen: Plädoyer für eine Ökologische Linke Opposition* (Hamburg: Carlsen Verlag, 1992), part three, especially pp. 158, 172. Ditfurth was formerly a leading spokesperson for the leftists in the German Greens. Now that the Greens have lost their radicalism, she is currently involved in organizing the Ecological Left (Ökologische Linke) in Frankfurt.

3. George L. Mosse, "The Mystical Origins of National Socialism," *Journal of the History of Ideas*, vol. 22, no. 1 (Jan. 1961), p. 81. See also Jeffrey A. Goldstein, "On Racism and Anti-Semitism in Occultism and Nazism," *Yad Vashem Studies* 13, Livia Rothkirchen, ed. (Jerusalem: Yad Vashem, 1979), pp. 53-72.

4. George L. Mosse, *The Crisis of German Ideology: Intellectual Origins of the Third Reich* (New York: Grosset and Dunlap, Universal Library, 1964), p. 4.

5. On the *völkisch* movement, see Mosse, *Crisis*; Fritz Stern, *The Politics of Cultural Despair: A Study in the Rise of the Germanic Ideology* (Berkeley and Los Angeles: University of California Press, 1961); and Walter Z. Laqueur, *Young Germany: A History of the German Youth Movement* (New York: Basic Books, 1962).

6. Quoted in Ditfurth, *Feuer*, p. 170.

7. Wolfgang Haug, "'Pogromen beginnen im Kopf,'" *Schwarzer Faden: Vierteljahresschrift für Lust und Freiheit* [Grafenau]; translated as "'Pogroms Begin in the Mind'" in *Green Perspectives*, no. 26 (May 1992).

8. Volkmar Wölk, "Neue Trends im ökofaschistischen Netzwerk: Am Beispiel der Anthroposophen, dem Weltbund zum Schutz des Lebens

und der ÖDP," in *In bester Gesellschaft: Antifa-Recherche zwischen Konservatismus und Neo-faschismus*, Raimund Hethey and Peter Kratz, eds. (Göttingen: Verlag die Werkstatt, 1991). Wölk is a spokesperson for the VVN/Bund of Antifascists and has published widely on 'neofascism.'

9. Unless otherwise indicated, quotations in this section are from the National Revolutionaries' documents *Gegen Fremdherrschaft und Kapital* and *Grundsätze unseres Wollens — Die fünffache Revolution* (n.d.), as cited in Ditfurth, *Feuer*, pp. 228-30.

10. Walter Laqueur, *Germany Today: A Personal Report* (Boston: Little, Brown, 1985), p. 152. Also on Strasserite ideology, see Mosse, *Crisis*, pp. 286-90.

11. See Hans-Georg Betz, "On the German Question: Left, Right, and the Politics of National Identity," *Radical America*, vol. 20, no. 1 (1987), pp. 30-48.

12. See Betz, "On the German Question."

13. Henning Eichberg, "Produktivistische Mythen: Etwas über die Religion in der Industriekultur," in *Zurück zur Natur-Religion?* Holger Schleip, ed. (Freiburg: Hermann Bauer Verlag, 1986). Editor Schleip is, ironically, a member both of the Greens and of the *völkisch*-racist sect Deutsche Unitarier; the publisher, Hermann Bauer Verlag, is the largest New Age publisher in Germany. The content of Eichberg's article is summarized in Wölk, "Neue Trends," p. 126.

14. Laqueur, *Germany Today*, p. 153. Laqueur cites Henning Eichberg, "Balkanisierung für jedermann," in the National Revolutionaries' periodical *Wir Selbst*, "a journal for national identity and international solidarity" (May-June 1983). The German right has been interested in the IRA since the 1920s; the title of this journal, *Wir Selbst* ("we ourselves"), is a translation of *Sinn Fein*.

15. See Betz, "On the German Question," pp. 45-46; and Wölk, "Neue Trends," p. 123.

16. Unless otherwise indicated, quotations in this section are from the FAP's Action Program (15 Aug. 1990); the FAP charter (15 Aug. 1989); "Basic Principles and Goals of the FAP — Electoral Program for Rhineland-Westphalia" (n.d.); and "Overview of Members of the Party Executive Committee for the Provincial Associations" (15 Aug. 1990), all as cited in Ditfurth, *Feuer*, p. 229ff. [Since early 1993, when this article was originally written, the FAP has been banned in the Federal Republic.]

17. See Christopher T. Husbands, "Militant Neo-Nazism in the Federal Republic of Germany in the 1960s," in *Neo-Fascism in Europe,* Luciano Cheles, Ronnie Ferguson, and Michalina Vaughan, eds. (Essex: Longman Group, UK Limited, 1991).

18. See Husbands, "Militant Neo-Nazism."

19. Husbands, "Militant Neo-Nazism," p. 96.

20. Quotations in this section are from the basic program of the Republicans, adopted at their first federal congress (26 Nov. 1983) in Munich; the 1987 program of the Republicans; "Ja zu Europa — Nein zu dieser EG — Deutsche Interessen haben Vorrang," the Dinkelsbühl Declaration of the Republicans for the European elections of 1979; and the 1990 party program of the Republicans, all as cited in Ditfurth, *Feuer,* p. 228ff.

21. Unless otherwise indicated, quotations in this section are from the NPD's 1973 Düsseldorf program; the 1988 *Wurfsendung* of the NPD; and the NPD newspaper *Deutsche Stimme* 4-5 (1992), all as cited in Ditfurth, *Feuer,* p. 228ff. On the NPD generally, see David Childs, "The Far Right in Germany Since 1945," in *Neo-Fascism in Europe,* Cheles, Ferguson, and Vaughan, eds.

22. Betz, "On the German Question," p. 35.

23. Quotations in this section are from a DVU leaflet (c. 1990) and "Overview of the Members of the Party Executive and the Provincial Associations" (20 Nov. 1989), as cited in Ditfurth, *Feuer,* p. 228ff.

24. The following section on the root-race theory is based on Wölk, "Neue Trends," pp. 120-21, and Ditfurth, *Feuer,* pp. 217-22. In English, a mild 'revised' account appears in Rudolf Steiner, *An Outline of Occult Science* (Spring Valley, N.Y.: Anthroposophical Press, 1972), especially chap. 6.

25. Rudolf Steiner, lecture (3 March 1923), *Gesamtausgabe,* vol. 349, pp. 52-67, cited in Ditfurth, *Feuer,* p. 221.

26. Steiner, *Outline,* p. 216.

27. Quoted in Ditfurth, *Feuer,* p. 216.

28. Quoted in Ditfurth, *Feuer,* p. 216.

29. Steiner, *Outline,* p. 361.

30. Ditfurth, *Feuer,* p. 200.

31. See Wölk, "Neue Trends," p. 123.

32. Ditfurth, *Feuer,* p. 222.

33. He is mentioned in passing in Laqueur, *Young Germany,* p. 194n.

34. Ditfurth, *Feuer,* p. 224.

35. Quoted in Betz, "On the German Question," p. 36.

36. Werner Georg Haverbeck, *Rudolf Steiner: Anwalt für Deutschland* (Munich, 1989), pp. 143f, 242f, 324, cited in Ditfurth, *Feuer*, pp. 224-26.

37. Werner Georg Haverbeck, "Das Ringen um Völker- und Geistesfreiheit," in *Europa* (Feb. 1990), p. 41f, cited in Wölk, "Neue Trends," pp. 131-32.

38. Wölk, "Neue Trends," p. 132.

39. Letter from the WSL's provincial executive for Schleswig-Holstein to the WSL presidium (28 July 1981), cited in Wölk, "Neue Trends," p. 133; also in *Vlothoer Tageblatt* (19 Nov. 1982), cited in Ditfurth *Feuer*, p. 225.

40. Ursula Haverbeck-Wetzel, "Vom Wirtschaftskrieg zum Geisteskampf," in *Europa* (Mar. 1990), p. 28, cited in Wölk, "Neue Trends," p. 132.

41. Helmut Roehrig, letter (2 Apr. 1982), cited in Wölk, "Neue Trends," p. 133.

42. Cited in Wölk, "Neue Trends," pp. 13-34. On Springmann in the Greens, see, e.g., Werner Hülsberg, *The German Greens: A Social and Political Profile*, trans. Gus Fagan (London and New York: Verso, 1988), pp. 94-95.

43. *Neue Anthropologie* 3-4 (1988), p. 91, cited in Wölk, "Neue Trends," p. 131.

44. Ditfurth, *Feuer*, p. 190.

45. See conversation with Rudolf Bahro, "Die deutschen Linken und die nationale Frage oder unsere Ölinteressen am Golf," *Streitschrift 3* (Nov. 1990), pp. 4-7; quoted in Ditfurth, *Feuer*, p. 210.

46. Conversation with Rudolf Bahro, *Streitschrift*, quoted in Roger Niedenführ, "New Age: Die spirituelle Rehabilitierung der Nationalsozialisten durch Rudolf Bahro, Rainer Langhans und J. Kirchoff," in *In bester Gesellschaft: Antifa-Recherche zwischen Konservatismus und Neo-faschismus*, Raimund Hethey and Peter Kratz, eds. (Göttingen: Verlag die Werkstatt, 1991), pp. 141-54, at 149.

47. Niedenführ, "New Age," pp. 141-54, esp. 147-50.

48. Quoted in Hülsberg, *German Greens*, p. 93.

49. See the exchange between Bahro and André Gorz in *Telos*, no. 51 (Spring 1982). See also Rudolf Bahro's *From Red to Green: Interviews with New Left Review*, trans. Gus Fagan and Richard Hurst (London: Verso, 1984), especially part three, wherein Bahro says, "In practice,

if we want to build an ecological decentralized Germany, we have to first free German territory" (p. 237).

50. Bahro, From *Red to Green*, pp. 220-21.

51. Rudolf Bahro, "Hinein oder hinaus? Wozu steigen wir auf? Rede auf der Bundesdelegiertenkonferenz der Grünen" (Hamburg), *Kommune* 1 (1985), pp. 40-43.

52. Conversation with Rudolf Bahro, "Die deutschen," *Streitschrift*, quoted in Ditfurth, *Feuer*, p. 210.

53. Rudolf Bahro, *Connection* (July-Aug. 1989), quoted in Ditfurth, *Feuer*, pp. 207-08.

54. Lernwerkstatt, *Rundbrief* 13 (c. 1990); the Lernwerkstatt's 1991 program.

55. Rudolf Bahro, *Logik der Rettung: Wer kann die Apokalypse aufhalten?* — *Ein Versuch über die Grundlagen ökologischer Politik* (Stuttgart and Vienna, 1987). I will refer to this book herein as *The Logic of Salvation*.

56. Conversation with Rudolf Bahro, "Die deutschen," *Streitschrift*, quoted in Ditfurth, *Feuer*, p. 210.

57. The author was present at this debate.

58. Rudolf Bahro, "Rette sich, wer kann," an interview with Rudolf Bahro, *Connection*, vol. 5, no. 8 (1989), pp. 18-19, cited in Niedenführ, "New Age," p. 148.

59. "Die Logik der Selbstausrottung," an interview with Rudolf Bahro, *Magazin 2000*, vol. 22, nos. 81-82 (1989), p. 64, cited in Niedenführ, "New Age," p. 148.

60. Niedenführ, "New Age," pp. 147-48.

61. Rudolf Bahro, "Lösung des Schattens und ökologische Kulturentwurf," *Connection*, vol. 6, no. 2 (1990), p. 65, cited in Niedenführ, "New Age," pp. 147-48.

62. Bahro, *Logik*, p. 153.

63. Bahro, *Logik*, p. 335; emphasis in the original.

64. Peter Kratz, "Bahros 'Grune Adolfs': Die 'Neue Rechte' an der Berliner Humboldt-Universität," reprinted in *A-Kurier* [Berlin] 41 (1993), pp. 6-15.

65. Bahro, *Logik*, p. 391.

66. Bahro, *Logik*, pp. 67-70. On the Conservative Revolution, see Stern, *Cultural Despair*, passim.

67. Conversation with Rudolf Bahro, "Die deutschen," *Streitschrift*, quoted in Ditfurth, *Feuer*, p. 210.

68. Kratz, "Bahros 'Grune Adolfs,'" p. 6.

69. Quoted in Dietmar Pieper, "Schickimicki unter Wolfen," *Der Spiegel* 26 (22 June 1992), pp. 62-63. See also Bahro, *Logik*, pp. 344, 481.

70. Rudolf Bahro, "Über kommunitäre Subsistenzwirtschaft und ihre Startbedingungen in die neuen Bundesländer," working paper, p. 10, cited in Kratz, "Bahros 'Grüne Adolfs,'" p. 9.

71. Bahro, *Logik*, p. 363.

72. "Salvation government" in Bahro, *Logik*; "god-state" in Pieper, "Schickimicki."

73. Bahro, *Logik*, p. 325.

74. Bahro, *Logik*, p. 491ff.

75. Bahro, *Logik*, p. 59.

76. Quoted in Ditfurth, *Feuer*, p. 206.

77. Conversation with Rudolf Bahro, "Die deutschen," *Streitschrift*, quoted in Kratz, "Bahros 'Grüne Adolfs,'" p. 8.

78. Bahro, *Logik*, p. 64.

79. Bahro, *Logik*, pp. 344-45.

80. Bahro, *Logik*, p. 346f. See also Robert Jungk, "Sein Kampf: Kritik an *Logik der Rettung*," in *tageszeitung* (10 Oct. 1987).

81. Bahro, *Logik*, p. 350.

82. Bahro, *Logik*, p. 461.

83. Bahro, *Logik*, p. 399.

84. Conversation with Rudolf Bahro, "Die deutschen," *Streitschrift*, p. 6, quoted in Kratz, "Bahros 'Grüne Adolfs,'" p. 8.

85. Conversation with Rudolf Bahro, "Die deutschen," *Streitschrift*, p. 6, quoted in Kratz, "Bahros 'Grüne Adolfs,'" p. 8.

86. Bahro, *Logik*, p. 347.

87. On the 'sleeping emperor,' see Norman Cohn, *The Pursuit of the Millennium: Revolutionary Millennarians and the Mystical Anarchists of the Middle Ages*, rev. ed. (London and New York: Oxford University Press, 1970; original, 1961), chaps. 6-7.

88. Summarized by Niedenführ, "New Age," p. 149ff.

89. Rudolf Bahro, foreword to Jochen Kirchhoff, *Nietzsche, Hitler und die Deutschen: Die Perversion des Neuen Zeitalters* (Berlin, 1990), quoted in Niedenführ, "New Age," p. 150.

90. Bahro, foreword to Kirchhoff, *Nietzsche, Hitler*, quoted in Niedenführ, "New Age," p. 150.

91. Niedenführ, "New Age," p. 150.

92. Bahro, *Logik*, p. 346.

93. Rudolf Bahro, *Rückkehr: Die In-Welt Krise als Ursprung der Weltzerstörung* (Frankfurt: Horizonte Verlag/Berlin: Altis Verlag, 1991), pp. 24-25.

94. All Langhans's quotes are from Niedenführ, "New Age," p. 146.

95. Bahro, foreword to Kirchhoff, *Nietzsche, Hitler*, p. 26, cited in Niedenführ, "New Age,"p. 152.

96. On Christophersen and Holocaust denial, see, for example, Roger Eatwell, "The Holocaust Denial: A Study in Propaganda Technique," in *Neo-Fascism in Europe*, Cheles, Ferguson, and Vaughan, eds.

97. This exchange was transcribed from a tape recording of the Bookchin-Bahro discussion, at which the author was present.

98. Quoted in Anti-EG Gruppe Köln, "Mit 'LebensschützerInnen' und RassistInnen gegen EG und Kolonialismus? Anmerkungen zur ÖDP und anderen 'BundnispartnerInnen' in der Kampagne '92," *ÖkoLinX: Zeitschrift der ökologischen Linken 6* (July-Aug.-Sept. 1992), pp. 11 and 19, translated into English as "Should We Work in Coalition with 'Right-to-Lifers' and Racists?" *Green Perspectives*, no. 27 (Aug. 1992), pp. 2-6.

99. Daniel Gasman, *The Scientific Origins of National Socialism: Social Darwinism in Ernst Haeckel and the German Monist League* (New York: American Elsevier; London: Macdonald & Co., 1971), pp. xxii-xxiii.

100. Adolf Hitler, *Mein Kampf*, trans. Ralph Mannheim (Boston: Houghton Mifflin, 1943), pp. 288, 400.

101. Gasman, *Scientific Origins*, p. xxiii.

102. For critiques of Gruhl, see: Anti-EG-Gruppe Köln, "Mit 'LebensschützerInnen'"; Antifa-Gruppe Freiburg und Volksfront gegen Reaktion, Faschismus und Krieg, eds., *Beitrag zur Kritik des Ökologismus* and *Beitrag zur Ideologie und Programmatik der ÖDP* (Cologne: GNN-Verlag, 1989); and Ditfurth, *Feuer*, pp. 151-69.

103. Herbert Gruhl, *Ein Planet wird geplündert* (reprint Frankfurt/ Main, 1987; original, 1975).

104. Charlene Spretnak and Fritjof Capra, *Green Politics* (New York: E. P. Dutton, 1984), p. 15.

105. Ditfurth, *Feuer*, p. 152.

106. See, e.g., *tageszeitung* (7 Nov. 1991).

107. Quoted in Antifa-Gruppe Freiburg, *Beitrag*, p. 30.

108. Herbert Gruhl, *Das irdische Gleichgewicht* (Munich, 1985), p. 127; Antifa-Gruppe Freiburg, *Beitrag*, p . 27; and Anti-EG Gruppe Köln, "Mit 'LebensschützerInnen,'" p. 10.

109. Quoted in Antifa-Gruppe Freiburg, *Beitrag*, p. 35.

110. Antifa-Gruppe Freiburg, *Beitrag*, p. 68.

111. Quoted in Ditfurth, *Feuer*, p. 159.

112. Gruhl, *Ein Planet*, p. 322f.

113. Quoted in Antifa-Gruppe Freiburg, *Beitrag*, p. 114f.

114. Quoted in Anti-EG Gruppe Köln, "Mit 'LebensschützerInnen,'" p. 11.

115. Herbert Gruhl, "Die Menschheit ist am Ende," *Der Spiegel* 13 (1992), pp. 57-58.

116. Quoted in Anti-EG Gruppe Köln, "Mit 'LebensschützerInnen,'" p. 11.

117. Quoted in Anti-EG Gruppe Köln, "Mit 'LebensschützerInnen,'" p. 10.

118. Gruhl, *Ein Planet*, p. 110.

119. Herbert Gruhl, *Himmelfahrt ins Nichts* (Munich: Verlag Langen Müller, 1992), p. 242. See Thomas Ebermann's criticism, "Massakriert den Armen!" *Konkret* (June 1991), pp. 36-37, translated into English as "Massacre the Poor!" *Green Perspectives*, no. 27 (Aug. 1992), pp. 6-7.

120. Quoted in Antifa-Gruppe Freiburg, *Beitrag*, p. 113.

121. Quoted in Reimar Paul, "EK III in Grün-Braun," *Konkret* [Hamburg] (Dec. 1991), pp. 35-36.

122. Quoted in Paul, "EK III," pp. 35-36.

123. Tom Metzger, quoted in Elinor Langer, "The American Neo-Nazi Movement Today," *Nation* (16-23 July 1990), pp. 82-107, at 86.

124. Quoted in Langer, "American Neo-Nazi Movement," p. 86.

125. Bill Devall, *Simple in Means, Rich in Ends: Practicing Deep Ecology* (Layton, UT: Gibbs Smith, 1988), p. 189.

A new CD recording from AK Press

NOAM CHOMSKY
THE CLINTON VISION

AK Audio, the newly formed audio imprint of AK Press, was created in order to bring the excitement and immediacy of the spoken word to people who care about politics. Reasonably priced, timely, and available on high-quality compact disc, **AK Audio** recordings deliver the best in political speech.

As an inaugural release, **AK Audio** makes Noam Chomsky, popular speaker, linguist, author, and political commentator, available to the home audience for the first time ever on compact disc. In 1992 Bill Clinton was elected President of the United States. After 12 years of a Republican White House, voters hungry for change believed Clinton when he promised a new vision, a new activism, and a new direction for the US. In **The Clinton Vision,** Noam Chomsky speaks about the US President's actions on NAFTA, health care, crime, labor relations, foreign policy, and the economy.

"Chomsky has been unrelenting in his attacks on the American hierarchy.... [He] is up there with Thoreau and Emerson in the literature of rebellion." — Rolling Stone

"If the job of a rebel is to tear down the old and prepare for the new, then this is Noam Chomsky, a 'rebel without a pause,' the 'Elvis of academia....' As rock 'n roll in the 90s continues to be gagged, it is ironic that a man of 65 years turns out to be the real rebel spirit." — U2's Bono

"How adroitly [Chomsky] cuts through the crap and actually says something." — Village Voice

ISBN 1-873176-92-9; $12.98/£10.99; CD; 56 minutes; two-color cover. **The Clinton Vision** CD is available direct from AK Press for $12.98/£10.99 ppd.

AK Friends
PRESS of AK Press

In the last 12 months, AK Press has published around 15 new titles. In the next 12 months we should be able to publish roughly the same, including new work by Murray Bookchin, CRASS, Daniel Guerin, Noam Chomsky, Jello Biafra, Stewart Home, a new anthology of situationist writings, new audio work from Noam Chomsky, plus more. However, not only are we financially constrained as to what (and how much) we can publish, we already have a huge backlog of excellent material we would like to publish sooner, rather than later. If we had the money, we could easily publish 30 titles in the coming 12 months.

Projects currently being worked on include a collection of essays by Nestor Makhno; previously unpublished early anarchist writings by Victor Serge; more work from Noam Chomsky, Murray Bookchin and Stewart Home; Raoul Vaneigem on the surrealists; a new anthology of computer hacking and hacker culture; a short history of British Fascism; the collected writings of Guy Aldred; a new anthology of cutting edge radical fiction and poetry; an updated version of the seminal anthology of contemporary anarchist writings, *Re-Inventing Anarchy*; new work from Freddie Baer; Albert Meltzer's autobiography and an updated reprint of *The Floodgates of Anarchy*; the autobiography and political writings of former Black Panther and class war prisoner Lorenzo Kom'boa Ervin, and much, much more. As well as working on the new AK Press Audio series, we are also working to set up a new pamphlet series, both to reprint long neglected classics and to present new material in a cheap, accessible format.

Friends of AK Press is a way in which you can directly help us try to realize many more such projects, much faster. Friends pay a minimum of $15/£10 per month into our AK Press account. All moneys received go directly into our publishing. In return, Friends receive (for the duration of their membership), automatically, as and when they appear, one copy free of every new AK Press title. Secondly, they are also entitled to 10 percent discount on everything featured in the current AK Distribution mail-order catalog (upwards of 3,000 titles), on any and every order. **Friends,** if they wish, can be acknowledged as a **Friend** in all new AK Press titles.

To find out more on how to contribute to Friends of AK Press, and for a Friends order form, please do write to:

AK Press	AK Press
PO Box 40682	22 Lutton Place
San Francisco, CA	Edinburgh, Scotland
94140-0682	EH8 9PE

Some Recent Titles from AK Press

WHICH WAY FOR THE ECOLOGY MOVEMENT by Murray Bookchin; ISBN 1 873176 26 0; 80pp two color cover, perfect bound 5-1/2 x 8-1/2; £4.50/$6.00. Bookchin attacks the misanthropic notions that the environmental crisis is caused mainly by overpopulation or humanity's genetic makeup. He points to the social and economic causes as the problem the environmental movement must deal with.

TO REMEMBER SPAIN: THE ANARCHIST AND SYNDICALIST REVOLUTION OF 1936 by Murray Bookchin; ISBN 1 873176 87 2; 80pp two color cover, perfect bound 5-1/2 x 8-1/2; £4.50/$6.00. These essays describe, analyze, and evaluate the last of the great proletarian revolutions of the past two centuries. A highly informative and theoretically significant assessment, drawing lessons for today about left-libertarian forms of organization and much-needed modifications of radical politics in the present period.

SOCIAL ANARCHISM OR LIFESTYLE ANARCHISM: AN UNBRIDGEABLE CHASM by Murray Bookchin; ISBN 1 873176 83 X; 96pp two color cover, perfect bound 5-1/2 x 8-1/2; £5.95/£7.95. A timely polemic against the purveyors of 'boutique anarchism' and a firm restatement of the classical, and sorely lacking, theory of class struggle anarchist practice. Includes the essay The Left That Was.

END TIME: NOTES ON THE APOCALYPSE by G.A. Matiasz; ISBN 1873176 96 1; 320 pp four color cover, perfect bound 5-1/2 x 8-1/2; £5.95/$7.00. A first novel by G.A. Matiasz, an original voice of slashing, thought provoking style. "A compulsively readable thriller combined with a very smart meditation on the near-future of anarchism, *End Time* proves once again that science fiction is our only literature of ideas." — Hakim Bey

ECSTATIC INCISIONS: THE COLLAGES OF FREDDIE BAER by Freddie Baer, preface by Peter Lamborn Wilson; ISBN 1 873176 60 0; 80 pages, a three color cover, perfect bound 8 1/2 x 11; £7.95/$11.95. This is Freddie Baer's first collection of collage work; over the last decade her illustrations have appeared on numerous magazine covers, posters, t-shirts, and album sleeves. Includes collaborations with Hakim Bey, T. Fulano, Jason Keehn, and David Watson.

STEALWORKS: THE GRAPHIC DETAILS OF JOHN YATES by John Yates; ISBN 1 873176 51 1; 136 pp two color cover, perfect bound 8-1/2 x 11; £7.95/$11.95. A collection to date of work created by a visual mechanic and graphic surgeon. His work is a mixture of bold visuals, minimalist to-the-point social commentary, involves the manipulation and reinterpretation of culture's media imagery.

AK Press publishes and distributes a wide variety of radical literature. For our latest catalog featuring these and several thousand other titles, please send a large self-addressed, stamped envelope to:

AK Press
22 Lutton Place
Edinburgh, Scotland
EH8 9PE, Great Britain

AK Press
P.O. Box 40682
San Francisco, CA
94140-0682